ISSN 2475-2061

Dediu Newsletter

Author: Michael M. Dediu

I0040940

World Monthly Report
News and Suggestions for Sustainable
Peace, Freedom and Prosperity

Vol. 5, Nr. 5 (53), 6 April 2021

DERC Publishing House
Nashua, New Hampshire, U. S. A.
For subscriptions, please use the contact form at www.derc.com

Published and printed in the
United States of America
On the Great Seal of the United States are included:
E Pluribus Unum (Out of many, one)
Annuit Coeptis (He has approved of the undertakings)
Novus Ordo Seclorum (New order of the ages)

Dediu, Michael M.

Dediu Newsletter Vol 5, Number 5 (53), 6 April 2021
World Monthly Report with news and suggestions for Sustainable Peace, Freedom and Prosperity

ISSN 2475-2061
ISBN 978-1-950999-35-4

Preface

Socrates, 433 BC: "The secret of change is to focus all your energy, not on fighting the old, but on building the new." – exactly this we are doing. The shortest route to growth and prosperity for all is to have peace, freedom, good health, good education, good jobs, good science & technology & culture, and harmony.

From a world sustainable peace, good health, freedom and prosperity point of view, this March 2021 had - beside the worrying news of great increases in war-related expenses and preparations – the still complicated COVID-19 pandemic continues to be a serious medical issue, but there are signs of improvement.

Now some good news: protein AEG12 strongly inhibits the family of viruses that cause yellow fever, dengue, West Nile, and Zika; Hominis is the first surgical robot with arms, designed to replicate the motions and capabilities of a surgeon's arms; Amazon.com is developing a chip to power the hardware switches used in networking; specialists want to transform cancer pathology with AI.

In this World Monthly Report, which is the 53rd in total, we included the most relevant news, in a balanced approach, usually directly from the source, to help the general public better understand the realities around us. Being well and correctly informed is a sine qua non requirement for everybody, in order to make the right decisions for the future. This World Monthly Report provides the information needed for making the best-informed decisions.

Enjoy this global, comprehensive, useful and timely World Monthly Report, and be optimist!

Michael M. Dediu, Ph. D.

Nashua, NH, U. S. A., 6 April 2021

On West 42nd Street at Fifth Avenue, looking southeast at Chrysler building (back up, Walter P. Chrysler (1875-1940), 1930, 319 m, 77 floors, 111,000 m^2 floor area, 32 elevators, at Lexington Avenue), before it is Grand Hyatt New York Hotel (1919, 90 m), and before it is Grand Central Terminal (1871, 1903, 1913, 2000, built by Cornelius Vanderbilt (1794-1877, the 2nd richest American, after John D. Rockefeller (1839-1937)) and his 13 children, commuter railroad terminal, with a grand façade and concourse, at Park Avenue, 47 acres, 44 high-level platforms, 67 tracks on 2 levels).

Table of Contents

Italy, Rome (753 BC, one of the oldest cities in Europe, called Roma Aeterna (The Eternal City) and Caput Mundi (Capital of the World)), from the Pincian Hill looking southwest: Piazza del Popolo (1822), with the Egyptian obelisk (36 m) of Sety I (1290–1279 BC) and Rameses II (1303, 1279–1213 BC) from Heliopolis, brought in 10 BC by Augustus (63 BC-14 AD) for Circus Maximus, in 1589 here. Basilica San Pietro (1506, 132 m, back).

World Status Report
3 April 2021

The World Constitution Day is 6 March.

Because the world digital environment is being used by international terrorists and organized crime, the International Information Security will be based on this cybersecurity for all: all computers will have a place for the user's card – the user's card will have the information about the user, will be registered (for a small fee) with the local cyber-police (which will be connected to the world cyber-police), and the user's card will appear on all the computers contacted by that user, and on user's e-mails. If something unfriendly comes from a computer, it's user card number will be given to the cyber-police, who will immediately contact the user for clarifications and – when necessary – for arrest. Shortly after the implementation of this simple and very efficient cybersecurity method, all computers and information systems will be very safe and friendly, how it was supposed to be from the beginning.

The current financial situation leads to a cycle of rising prices, higher interest rates and a ballooning debt.

The future belongs to people who want and work for peace, freedom, good health, good education, good jobs, good science & technology, harmony and prosperity for all.

3 March is World Hearing Day - the first World Report on Hearing is a significant milestone for hearing health care around the world. Released by the World Health Organization to coincide with World Hearing Day, the report underscores the broad and profound public health consequences that unaddressed hearing loss has on societies worldwide. Informed by international public health experts, the report aims to mobilize a coordinated and sustained

global response, based on scientific best practices, to prioritize and improve access to patient-centered ear and hearing care. Also, all noisy equipment must be made much less noisy, using advanced technology.

The medical device supply chains need intense work of modernization.

It is necessary that for many situations, including sporting events, urgent care clinics, ambulances, and schools, people will have on hand the blood test system for traumatic brain injury.

More than 25% of the adults age 65+ are socially isolated – the governments and private organizations must help.

The acceptance by the people of destructive, abusive and arbitrary rules, restrictions, and mandates is not good – the people should calmly and politely explain that these things are not appropriate for a civilized society.

International research teams are the future of research and development.

Cardiovascular diseases are one of the top killers globally. Biotech companies around the world are investigating ways to take down these deadly conditions using technology, such as bio-additive manufacturing, and artificial hearts.

International economic cooperation should be free and intense, for the benefit of all people.

From a political point of view, the people of the world will integrate all political parties in a World Popular Association for Peace, Freedom, Health, Education, Jobs, Harmony and Prosperity for All (WOPAPEFEHEJOHAPQA, or shortly WOPAP). When this WOPAP achieves its goal of implementing the World Constitution in a few short years, it will dissolve itself with great satisfaction, and all people will enjoy good, healthy and harmonious life.

Nuclear energy – not for nuclear bombs, but for peaceful use - is one of the greatest energy sources available to the world.

People will create a better future with the new World Constitution.

Market generally means a few thousands of professional traders and speculators, who manipulate many billions of shares to their advantage.

There is a sharp acceleration in inflation and deficit.
Because of the fiat (from Latin "let it be done") money (not backed by gold), central banks print money as they want.

March is the World Kidney Month.
Chronic kidney disease (CKD) is a serious condition affecting 37 millions of U.S. adults, over 800 millions in the world, and is often overlooked until symptoms appear.

11 March 2021. One year ago, the World Health Organization declared the COVID-19 outbreak a pandemic – all people extend gratitude to doctors, medical assistants, and other essential workers who helped keep things running.

Faster money printing is not good.

The sinews of the World Government will be very strong and clear.

Medical assistance is not one size fits all – each person needs a customized medical assistance.

People support the companies which decided to resolve any disputes by individual arbitration, and not by jury trial or class action.

14 March is π (Pi) Day.

Every family's needs are different, and there must be many different resources available to help.

The only enemies are viruses, bad bacteria, and all illnesses.

People ask to stop the abusive change of clocks twice a year, which create many health and other problems.

The miseducation is a big issue in the world.

Less than 20% of the world's population now live in a free country, but freedom advances every day.

March is vision month.

Global healthcare digitalization must have good standards.

20 March 2021 – March Equinox at 5:37 AM (the center of the Sun passed the Earth equatorial plane from south to north); also, this is the International Day of Happiness (this will be extended to all the days of the year).

The world's biggest natural capital assets are water, air, and vegetation.

The new World Constitution will bring a fortunate stroke of serendipity for all.

Complaint handling and solving is a major task for the world government.

There are still many sick people with some power, and they try to make other people sick too, but the people will soon correct these issues, and have the proper medical treatment for all.

A Connected Global Healthcare System is an urgent necessity.

All people are citizens of the Earth by birth, and then also citizens of their local countries.

While there are still too many preparations for war, there are also too many not-freedom oriented decisions, and too many not-friendly activities (instead of friendly discussions to solve the disagreements) - all people want peace, no arms, freedom, good health, good education, good jobs, harmony and prosperity for all.

Some sick individuals insult people, instead of discussing in a civilized and polite manner – people ask for medical assistance for those sick individuals.

With enough time, energy and money anything can be done for the benefit of all people.

Bureaucracy is an ugly mechanism operating very slowly, which destroys initiative, and all sound work.

MD Formula for Evaluation of work:
Evaluation of work = Quality * (Complexity & Magnitude of Work) / (Cost * Duration)
Quality is a number between 1 and 100 (best quality)
(Complexity & Magnitude of Work) is a number between 1 and 100 (very complex and big)
Cost in dollars, minimum $1
Duration = End Time – Start Time, in hours, minimum 0.1 hours.

30 March is the International Doctors' Day.

Small conflicts sabotage people's efforts for peace.

Difficult conversations must be assisted by medical personnel.

Space exploration and innovation are important for all people.

Scientific information related areas, including artificial intelligence, machine learning and advanced mathematical algorithms, are very important for the future.

Socrates: "The secret of change is to focus all your energy, not on fighting the old, but on building the new." – exactly this we are doing.

Important World Congress: the 7th World Congress of Smart Materials 2022 (WCSM2022)-Singapore, which will be held in Singapore from June 15-17, 2022.

There are many global challenges – they can be solved if all people have peace, freedom, good health, good education, good jobs, good science & technology, harmony and prosperity for all.

People make errors all the time – including the error of blaming something else for their errors. Corrective actions are necessary.

Many people in the world suffer from sickness, hunger, unemployment, bureaucratic mismanagement, and isolation, but soon these issues will be solved using the Constitution of the World.

Many global regulatory requirements are bad for people.

Harmony will soon replace conflicts everywhere.

All people emphasize the need for a medical global response to current medical situation.

Reports: Cryptocurrency is not good for people – it is mostly used by criminals, has suspicious origins, and it is manipulated by speculators.

The future of the people on Earth will de decentralized and self-managed.

In many countries, disinformation and misinformation are used to excuse incompetence and punish opposition.

Peace, pioneering spirit, freedom and hard work will be the base of Peaceful Terra.

The prevalence of neurological diseases has increased rapidly, and they are now the second biggest cause of death globally. With the search for treatments and cures proving difficult, change is needed, and better disease modeling will help.

Many bad things are happening every day in the world, to the detriment of many people, because sick people are not under medical treatment.

Global debt soars to 356% of GDP.

Hard and useful work is the base for good life and growth.

Patient-initiated and doctor-initiated visits, video, voice or e-mail sessions are very important for better health and for saving lives.

Work from home will be expanded in the world.

Inflation is a serious problem on the planet.

William Shakespeare – "One touch of nature makes the whole world kin."

The determination of all people to have peace, freedom, good health, good education, harmony and prosperity for all, is growing every day.

The world financial system is not safe, not stable and not sound.

Self-improvement is essential - Marcus Aurelius (26 April 121, Rome, Italy – 17 March 180, (58.9) Vindobona, now in Austria,

Roman emperor for 19 years from 161 to 180 and a Stoic philosopher. one of the great rulers of the Roman Empire), sets forth a series of self-reflective essays intended as a guide for his own self-improvement.

In the world there are many reasoning errors, false belief, knowledge corruption, and impeded learning, and much effort is necessary to correct the issues.

If You Want Peace, Prepare for Peace! – this is a well-known book (please see Bibliography). Also, If You Want Peace, Study Peace! All people applaud Colleges which are turning against the history of military conflict, because by studying peace students will be prepared for peace, while the wars will be mentioned as a very bad part of the history, not to be forgotten, and never to be repeated. Studying war, brings war – studying peace, brings peace.

All people must get the medical care they need, at home.

Water purification and recycling is an essential world project.

Self-discipline is a strict requirement for everybody.

Healthy planet means healthy people, no arms (which pollute everything), healthy land and healthy oceans (which are 71% of Earth's surface).

Individual responsibility is very important for all people on Earth.

Artificial intelligence must be used for the benefit of all people, not for killing people.

Fiscal responsibility is a first priority for all.

The global arms market will be transformed in the global medical and life-improving market.

The role of the state is to maintain peace, freedom, good health, good education, harmony, no abuses, balanced budget, no arms, friendly and clean elections, and prosperity.

Sustainable peace can be achieved only by eliminating all arms.

Ronald Reagan, State of the Union Address, 1984: "A nuclear war cannot be won and must never be fought. The only value, in our two nations possessing nuclear weapons, is to make sure they will never be used. But then would it not be better to do away with them entirely."

Thomas Jefferson (1743 - 1826) - "Rightful liberty is unobstructed action according to our will within limits drawn around us by the equal rights of others. I do not add 'within the limits of the law' because the law is often but the tyrant's will, and always so when it violates the right of an individual."

People want a global rethinking of priorities, focusing on peace, freedom, health, education, harmony and prosperity for all.

The world economic outlook is not good now – much more effort should be allocated to improve it.

Global Financial Stability Report: not good, too much deficit, not enough jobs, too much war-related expenses.

Fiscal Monitor: printing too much money.

Global economy should be focused on helping people, not on more arms to kill them.

People applaud the global organizations which work to improve the quality of life for many people on the planet.

The Sun – and our whole solar system - orbits around the center of the Milky Way Galaxy. We are moving at an average velocity of 230 km/sec, and it takes us about 230 millions of years to make one complete orbit around the Milky Way. This rotation around the center of the Milky Way Galaxy, at 230 km/s, creates the sinusoidal climate changes often observed on Earth.

Important for all countries: over 60 years ago, in Dwight D. Eisenhower's farewell speech, on January 17, 1961, the former famous Five Star General in the Army, Supreme Commander of the Allied Forces in Europe in World War II, and the 34th President of the United States warned of the dangers of allowing a Military-Industrial Complex to take control: "In the councils of government, we must guard against the acquisition of unwarranted influence, whether sought or unsought, by the military–industrial complex". The Military-Industrial Complex is a term that denotes an interdependent relationship between a nation's military, economy, and politics, and it is valid for all nations.

Everywhere in the world mediation should be a much better alternative to the courts.

Jefferson reminds all people: "All tyranny needs to gain a foothold is for people of good conscience to remain silent."

People remember Thucydides: Ignorance is bold and knowledge reserved.
And Leonardo da Vinci: Nothing strengthens authority so much as silence.

Over 360,000 babies are born each day in the world, over 130 M per year.

People ask to have AI, satellites and space used only for peaceful purposes.
Global security is real only if there are no arms at all.
World quality of life index: 2.1 (bad) (1 very bad, 10 excellent)
World medical assistance index: 2 (bad) (1 very bad, 10 excellent)
The State of Communications in World Healthcare - Broken
World noise level: unhealthy
World Financial Stability Index: 2 (1 very bad, 10 excellent)
World Food Stability Index: 3 (1 very bad, 10 excellent)
World Freedom Stability Index: 2 (1 very bad, 10 excellent)

Electrical Safety Standards Worldwide – good
Business Expectations Index – low
Business Uncertainty Index – high
- Global inflationary overheating is taking place.
- Saving Humanity from war is a major objective for the 7.7 B people on Earth.

The world borderlands are always in danger, with many conflicts every single day.

Misinformation, disinformation and mal-information are everywhere in the world these days.

Fiscal irresponsibility is very common these days.

Paris: Rue Soufflot (from Panthéon, looking north-west to Jardin du Luxembourg (1612, back), and Tour Eiffel (1889, 324 m)), with the Université Paris 1 Panthéon-Sorbonne (1150, 1971, right).

United States of America

(Population 330 M, rank 3, growth 0.5%. Free: 89 of 100. Area 9.52 M km^2, rank 4.).

Short Status Report:

27 February 2021. Janssen COVID-19 vaccine - the single-shot vaccine is the third COVID-19 vaccine in the United States to be granted an EUA. FDA approved Johnson & Johnson's (JNJ) COVID-19 shot, which was the third jab to be approved in the U.S. It's the first to have a single-dose regimen. The decision clears the way for immediate distribution and vaccination of the Janssen vaccine to Americans 18 and older, building on a broader rollout that's currently utilizing jabs from Pfizer/BioNTech and Moderna. The single-shot product had an overall efficacy rate of about 66% in the Phase 3 clinical trial, and the U.S. arm of the trial showed an efficacy rate of about 72%, and of 85% when protecting against severe or critical disease

Reports: More than 41,500 people were killed in shooting incidents across the United States in 2020, an average of more than 110 a day, and there were 592 mass shootings nationwide, an average of more than 1.6 a day. All people send condolences to the relatives and friends of the victims, and ask for serious measures to stop these killings.

According to a recent survey, 63% of late teens and young adults reported symptoms of anxiety or depression, 25% of which reported increased substance use to deal with the stress.

Reports: Seizures of methamphetamine and marijuana rose during pandemic. Findings suggest that the pandemic may have impacted the availability and demand of some, but not all, illegal drugs.

Reports: In Feb 2021 there were over 34,000 job cuts.

4 March 2021. Nonfarm business sector labor productivity decreased 4.2% in the fourth quarter of 2020, the U.S. Bureau of Labor Statistics reported today, as output increased 5.5% and hours worked increased 10.1%. (All quarterly percent changes in this release are seasonally adjusted annual rates.)

The Fed Balance Sheet on 25 Feb 2021 was over $7.6 T – normal is zero.

Reports: February 2021 – unemployment rate is 6.2%.
The U.S. remain 9.9 M jobs short of their pre-pandemic employment level, while about 18 M Americans are on some form of unemployment aid.
The monetary policy (very bad easy money) is wrong, and inflation continue to rise.
January US imports ($260.2 B) were the highest on record – trade deficit $68.2 B.
Total consumer credit outstanding is over $4.17 T (normal is less than $1 B)

Reports: Like in many other countries, throughout the midsection of the United States in February, record frigid temperatures were recorded, with some calling it global cooling, how was also declared about 30 years ago. Global cooling is already here, some say – look at Bismarck, North Dakota, where temperatures fell to decades-low numbers, or in Chicago, Oklahoma City, Dallas or Houston. San Antonio had snow for the first time in recent memory.

Reports: Democrat Senators Joe Manchin (D-WV) and Kyrsten Sinema (D-AZ) have publicly declared they're opposed to changing Senate rules to end the filibuster.

Reports: The Government Accountability Office's (GAO) 2021 high-risk list warned that federal human capital management, U.S. Postal Service (USPS) financial management, and cybersecurity problems are only getting worse. The new report identified 36 areas across government with "vulnerabilities to fraud, waste, abuse and mismanagement".

Reports: The sheer scale of the spending of $1.9 T will lead to a spike in inflation, as well as in deficit.

Only $75 B (7% of the $1.9 T price tag) are directed at COVID testing, contact tracing and vaccine distribution.

Americans that earned between $35,000 and $75,000 annually traded stocks about 90% more than the week prior to receiving their stimulus check, therefore a lot of that stimulus money will end up in the stock market, mostly to the benefit of speculators.

Bad news: More than half of the kids in America currently play games instead of learning.

February deficit: $311 B
Oct – Feb deficit: $1.047 T
FY 2020 deficit: $ 3.131 T
February 2020: U.S. debt $23.3 T

A report issued by the Federal Reserve found that about 40% of the Americans do not have $400 for unexpected expenses.

Reports: Democrat Senator Manchin does not agree with the halting of the Keystone XL Pipeline.

In February, total industrial production decreased 2.2%. Manufacturing output and mining production fell 3.1% and 5.4%, respectively; the output of utilities increased 7.4%.

Printing money is over $120 B/month.

Fed balance sheet is over $7.7 T ($1.000/world-person) – it should be zero.

Reports: The U.S. has been overwhelmed at the Mexico border in recent months, with the number of migrants attempting to enter the country tracking toward a 20-year high. The 100,441 encountered last month was the highest tally since March 2019.

The Federal Reserve estimates that about one-third of Americans - approximately 76 millions of adults - are just getting by, and don't have savings for unexpected expenses.

Bad news: A new poll from Mizuho Securities found that two out of five stimulus check recipients plan to invest at least some part of the proceeds into Bitcoin and stocks.

Fed: An increasing number of firms anticipate higher inflation in the coming year.

In 2020, U.S. businesses exported $1.431 T in goods and services to countries around the world. Nearly 75% of these sales went to just 15 countries.

Reports: Two out of every three of us are overweight or obese. Diabetes and high blood pressure are on the rise. Heart attacks, strokes, and cancer are distressingly common. Many factors contribute to these complex problems, but the basic reasons are simple: we eat too much, we choose the wrong foods, and we don't get enough exercise.

The U.S. current account trade deficit widened by $7.6 B, or 4.2%, to $188.5 B in the fourth quarter of 2020, according to statistics from the U.S. Bureau of Economic Analysis. The revised third quarter deficit was $180.9 B. The fourth quarter trade deficit was 3.5% of current dollar gross domestic product, up from 3.4% in the third quarter. Annual trade deficit 2020 -$647.2 B, 2019: -$480.2 B.

Reports: There was a second U.S. mass shooting (in Colorado, 10 people killed, after Atlanta, 8 people killed - other 18 victims added to the over 7 millions of people killed over the years by sick people with guns) in less than a week. All people ask for the elimination of all arms – people's life must be protected.

Reports: The U.S. now accounts for about 12% of global semiconductor manufacturing capacity, down from 37% in 1990.

Reports: 11.1% of families are homeschooling.

Reports: Stock trading is based on politics.

Very bad news: The New York State Senate and Assembly approved a bill that would legalize marijuana for recreational use. The Senate vote was 40-23 and the Assembly vote was 100-49. Marijuana is bad for people.

The third president of the United States, Thomas Jefferson, said about 195 years ago, in 1825: "I know no safe depository of the ultimate powers of the society but the people themselves. This is the true corrective of abuses of constitutional power."

People support deficit-concerned Democrat Senators, like West Virginia's Joe Manchin and Montana's Jon Tester.

Abusive and manipulative trading activities, and the opaque dealings of the market makers are taking place daily.

Health insurance increased by over 5.2% in 2021.

American manufacturers are increasingly turning to the international marketplace for opportunity and diversification.

Reports: Charter schools have 3.3 millions of students enrolled at 7,500 schools in 44 different states.

Many companies trade at a hyper-inflated 74 times earnings – normal is less than 2 times.

Very bad news: U.S. have world's highest rate of children living in single-parent households.

The 280-megahertz spectrum is especially important to wireless companies.

People's payment for electricity increased in 2021 by over 4.8%.

People want to receive 5% on their savings in banks, not to be forced to bet on horses, companies, fraudulent coins, etc.

Reports: Big shot companies and speculators take advantage of the easy money sloshing around in financial markets.

The fourth president of the United States from 1809 to 1817, James Madison, said about 190 years ago, in 1830: "The means of defense agst. foreign danger, have been always the instruments of tyranny at home."
"The advancement and diffusion of knowledge is the only guardian of true liberty."

Over 10,000 babies are born each day in the U.S., over 3.6 M per year.

Ballooning budget deficit and ballooning stock market go hand in hand.

- Financial responsibility is very low.
- Current overall inflation: 5.89%. It is high, under pressure, and expected to grow to 6.75 %.
- Credit risk is high.
- Market risk is very high.
- Asset prices are artificially inflated.
- Violent crimes are rising annually
- People should receive 5% interest for their deposits in banks.
- Economic outlook: unfavorable
- There is no Internet in 15% of the U.S. homes – 1 in 7 homes is without Internet.
There are 44.5 millions of seniors on Social Security.
Because of the production and sales of arms, mass shootings continue, and thousands of people are killed and wounded each year.

Puerto Rico: (Population 3.6 M, rank 134, decrease 0.1%; an unincorporated territory of the United States, located in the northeast Caribbean Sea, 1,600 km southeast of Miami, Florida.).

United Nations. (UN) There are 195 officially recognized countries. Around 44,000 people work for the United Nations. There is a wide range of jobs: Researchers, IT-specialists, lawyers, experts on finance and administration, or translators work at the New York headquarters, at the official locations, or at specialized agencies. More than half of the UN's workforce is employed in the field, in projects of humanitarian aid, or on peace missions.

World Trade Organization

G20 group members are European Union (EU) and 19 countries: Argentina, Australia, Brazil, Canada, China, France, Germany, India, Indonesia, Italy, Japan, Mexico, Republic of Korea, Republic of South Africa, Russia, Saudi Arabia, Turkey, United Kingdom, United States of America.

The Group of Seven (G7) is a group consisting of Canada, France, Germany, Italy, Japan, the United Kingdom, and the United States. The G8 format (the G7 and Russia) had been in place for 16 years, from 1998-2014.

China, Japan, and neighbors

China: (Population 1.4 B, rank 1, growth 0.4%. Freedom House reports for 2020: Not Free (10 of 100). Area 9.59 M km^2, rank 3).

Reports: One of the most powerful businessmen in the world is Jack Ma - the founder of e-commerce colossus Alibaba - but he's found himself at odds with the Chinese government. After he criticized Chinese-state owned banks last year, Beijing retaliated with an antitrust investigation into Alibaba, and pulled the listing of Ant Group, set to be the world's biggest IPO, in which Alibaba owns a one-third stake. The financial payments powerhouse, which is also China's largest holder of consumer credit information, has defied intense government pressure by only giving a small amount of financial data to the country's central bank, *FT* reports. Personal credit information is a so-called "public good," according to the PBOC, and should be kept by a publicly owned entity or government agency. The central bank has long wanted to create a pool of credit data to help state-owned banks gauge creditworthiness due to increasing consumer loan defaults. Ant is China's largest holder of consumer credit data, while its Alipay app is the country's biggest payments platform. The company, along with retail behemoth Alibaba, has seen Jack Ma become China's richest person, though he lost the title this week as his business empire came under regulatory scrutiny. Ant will likely cave in because, after all, it is a Chinese company, and must listen to the government to stay in business. But Ma's fight with the authorities is another example of the escalating tensions between the state and China's private sector, as President Xi exerts tighter control over the economy. Another area to consider is consumer trust in Ant Group, with many clients complaining online that they will walk away if their credit info is reported to the government.

Note. People kindly ask President Xi to focus on better relations with the business community, as well as on peace, freedom, good health, good education, good jobs, good science & technology, harmony and prosperity for all.

21 February 2021. Reports: China's Ministry of Agriculture and Rural Affairs (MARA) notified the U.S. Embassy in Beijing that on 4 February 2021, China detected highly pathogenic avian influenza (HPAI) H5N8 subtype in wild birds in a scenic area in Lianyungang City. China also notified this HPAI outbreak to the World Organization for Animal Health (OIE), and is monitoring the situation.

5 March 2021. Xinhua: China aims to expand its economy by over 6% in 2021, building on strong tailwind from success in containing COVID-19, as lawmakers gather in Beijing to map out priorities for high-quality development. The gross domestic product (GDP) target is one of the many key goals laid out in a government work report, delivered by Premier Li Keqiang, to the national legislature, which began its annual session Friday, 5 March.

"In setting this target, we have taken into account the recovery of economic activity," Li said. "A target of over 6% will enable all of us to devote full energy to promoting reform, innovation, and high-quality development."

This year, the country aims to create more than 11 millions of new urban jobs, lower the deficit-to-GDP ratio to 3.2%, and expand domestic demand and effective investment, which are expected to put the economy firmly back to pre-pandemic vibrancy -- China's GDP growth rate was 6% in 2019.

In 2021, China will pursue high-quality development, advance supply-side structural reform, and consolidate and expand the achievements of the COVID-19 response and economic and social development, among other major tasks outlined in the report.

"These efforts will enable us to get off to a good start in the 14th Five-Year Plan (2021-2015) period and commemorate the centenary of the Communist Party of China with outstanding achievements in development," Li said in the report, amid rounds of applause in the Great Hall of the People.

Reports: The Chinese National Congress has officially convened its "Two Sessions" annual parliamentary gathering, which sets economic and political priorities for 2021. The meeting took on additional importance this year as it marked the beginning of China's five-year development plan (the 14th in its history), as well as the 100th anniversary of the ruling Communist Party. Premier Li Keqiang said the country would target GDP growth of 6% or more this year, a figure that was lower than most economists' expectations of around 8%. It's also surprising given that it was the only major world economy to grow in 2020. China recovered relatively quickly from the initial coronavirus outbreak centered in the Chinese city of Wuhan, and ended up with 2.3% growth for the year. However, Chinese leaders scrapped a five-year GDP target, saying only that they would plan to keep the economy running "within a reasonable range." In the 2016-20 plan, the target was "more than 6.5%." Instead, they are aiming to cap the surveyed urban unemployment rate at 5.5%, with labor productivity growth outpacing overall GDP growth. The county also plans to increase its urbanization rate to 65%, from 60.6% in 2019. The conservative GDP growth targets indicate more restrained monetary and fiscal policies are coming in 2021 (contrast that with the U.S.). Policymakers have further put a recent focus on reining in debt and combating an emerging bubble in the real estate market. In the annual report, the government also said it would seek to cut the fiscal deficit target to 3.2% of projected GDP this year (vs. 3.6% in 2020, normal should be zero), and plans to reduce the amount of debt raised by local governments.

Reports: The Chinese pharmaceutical research and manufacturing company WuXi AppTec has acquired the UK CRO Oxgene in a move to gain its first European facility for developing and manufacturing gene therapies. According to the deal, Oxgene will become a subsidiary of WuXi AppTec's cell and gene therapy arm, WuXi Advanced Therapies.

7 March 2021. Xinhua: President Xi Jinping on Saturday, 6 March, stressed giving "strategic priority" to safeguarding people's health, and building a high-quality and balanced basic public education service system.

Note: People appreciate the attention on "giving "strategic priority" to safeguarding people's health, and building a high-quality and balanced basic public education service system", and kindly ask President Xi Jinping to focus on working for peace, zero arms, freedom, good health, good education, good jobs, good science & technology, harmony and prosperity for all.

10 March 2021. Xinhua: President Xi Jinping Tuesday, 9 March, stressed achieving a good start in strengthening national defense and the armed forces during the 14th Five-Year Plan (2021-2025) period. Xi, also general secretary of the Communist Party of

China Central Committee and chairman of the Central Military Commission, made the remarks while attending a plenary meeting of the delegation of the People's Liberation Army and People's Armed Police Force, at the fourth session of the 13th National People's Congress, the top legislature.

Addressing the meeting, Xi praised the whole armed forces for achieving the targets and missions for 2020 amid the COVID-19 epidemic and complex domestic and international circumstances.

Laying down requirements for ensuring the good start in the military development for the next five years, Xi said development of the armed forces must focus on combat readiness.

Xi demanded efforts to step up building high-caliber strategic deterrence and joint operation systems.

Underlining innovation-driven military development, Xi called for intensified efforts and more concrete measures in the pursuit of independent innovation in science and technology, to fully leverage the role of science and technology as the strategic support for military development. Innovation in defense-related science and technology must be significantly boosted, he said.

Highlighting the "instabilities" and "uncertainties" in China's current security circumstances, Xi said the whole armed forces must always be ready to respond to all kinds of complex and difficult situations, resolutely safeguard national sovereignty, security, and development interests, and provide strong support for fully building a modern socialist country.

Note: People are really concerned and very sad to see statements like these:

- "development of the armed forces must focus on combat readiness." Combat against whom? Is this a preparation for war?

- "to fully leverage the role of science and technology as the strategic support for military development. Innovation in defense-related science and technology must be significantly boosted". Why? Are science and technology used for war instead of peace? Does "a modern socialist country" mean a war-oriented country?

People kindly ask President Xi to clarify these questions, and to continue to focus on peace, no arms, freedom, good health, good education, good jobs, good science & technology (NOT for war!), harmony and prosperity for all.

Note: There are discussions between the U. S., China and Russia – all people, from all countries, kindly ask all leaders to focus on peace, no arms, freedom, good health, good education, good jobs, good science & technology (NOT for war!), harmony and prosperity for all.

20 March 2021. From Xinhua, with additions: Chang'e 5 orbiter, launched on 24 Nov. 2020, has successfully entered the First Lagrange (L1, Joseph-Louis Lagrange (Giuseppe Luigi Lagrangia 25 Jan 1736, Torino, Italia – 10 April 1813, Paris, France, 77.2), Italian mathematician and astronomer, later naturalized French) Point of the Sun-Earth system, the Beijing Aerospace Control Center said, adding that it is also China's first spacecraft to enter the First Lagrange Point's exploration orbit. The center on Thursday, 18 March, said the orbiter is 936,700 km from the Earth, and working normally with stable attitude and balanced power. It will operate in the exploration orbit of First Lagrange Point of Sun-Earth system with orbital period of about six months. The orbiter separated from the returner on Dec. 17, 2020, and started the long-term management phase on Dec. 21.

The orbiter had spent about 88 days to move to the First Lagrange Point of Sun-Earth system after undertaking two orbit maneuvers, and two mid-course corrections under the surveillance and control of the team. The spacecraft long-term management team is also in charge of daily management of Chang'e-3 lander, the lander and the rover of the Chang'e-4 probe, the relay satellite Queqiao (Magpie Bridge), and Tianwen-1 Mars probe, which are all operating in good condition. The First Lagrange Point of the Sun-Earth system is located on the connecting line between the Sun and the Earth, about 1.5 millions of kilometers from the Earth. This is the gravitationally dynamic equilibrium point between the Earth and the Sun.

It is easier for spacecraft to maintain a relatively stable running state and save fuel at the First Lagrange Point of the Sun-Earth system, which is also the best position for the solar observatory to continuously observe the Sun and the sunny side of the Earth.

8 March 2021. Reports: China's Ministry of Agriculture and Rural Affairs (MARA) notified the U.S. Embassy in Beijing that on March 2, 2021, China detected African Swine Fever (ASF) in live hogs transported into Yunnan Province. China notified this ASF

outbreak to the World Organization for Animal Health (OIE) and is continuing to monitor the situation.

Hong Kong. (Population 7.3 M, rank 104, growth 0.8%. Partly Free: 61 of 100).

Macau (Population 622 K, rank 167, growth 1.7 %.)

Taiwan: (Population 23.6 M, rank 56, growth 0.3%. Free, 91 of 100).

Japan (Population 127.5 M, rank 11, decrease 0.2%. Free, 96 of 100).

Afghanistan: (Population 35.5 M, rank 40, growth 2.5%. Not free: 24 of 100).

19 March 2021. Xinhua: Russia, China, the United States and Pakistan signed a joint statement on Thursday, 18 March, calling on all parties to the conflict in Afghanistan to reduce the level of violence, and urging the Taliban not to pursue a spring offensive. The statement on a peaceful settlement in Afghanistan was released by the Russian Foreign Ministry after a regular meeting of the four countries, or the extended "Troika," with the participation of representatives of the Afghan government and the Taliban.

Russia, China, the United States and Pakistan in the 10-point statement asked all Afghans to ensure that terrorist groups and individuals do not use Afghan soil to threaten the security of any other country. The four countries called on participants in the intra-Afghan negotiations to engage immediately in discussions on fundamental issues to resolve the conflict.

"At this pivotal moment, our four states call on the parties to negotiate and conclude a peace agreement that will bring an end to over four decades of war in Afghanistan," the statement read.

Note: All people support this joint statement, and kindly ask the 4 countries to invite many more countries to discuss and implement peace on Earth.

Reports: Terrorist attacks continue – the solution is an intense demilitarization of Afghanistan, all arms prohibited, major increase of medical personnel (to visit and register all people), businesses, teachers and police, national and local calm and friendly elections every year, national referenda every 3 months, heavy UN civilian assistance.

South Korea: (Population 50.9 M, rank 27, growth 0.4%. Free, 82 of 100).

Reports: Researchers at the Korea Advanced Institute of Science and Technology have invented a smartphone-controlled soft brain implant that can be recharged wirelessly from outside the body. It enables long-term neural circuit manipulation without the need for periodic surgeries to replace the implant's battery. Scientists believe it can help treat psychiatric disorders and neurodegenerative diseases.

North Korea: (Population 25.4 M, rank 52, growth 0.5%. Not free: 3 of 100).

Vietnam (Population 95.5 M, rank 15, growth 1%. Not free, 20 of 100, Socialist Republic of Vietnam).

Laos (Population. 6.8 M, rank 106, growth 1.5%. Not free: 12 of 100).

Cambodia (Population 16 M, rank 71, growth 1.5%. Not Free 31 of 100).

Mongolia (Population 3 M, rank 137, growth 1.6%. Free 85 of 100)

Nepal: (Population 29.3 M, rank 48, growth 1.1%. Partly free 52 of 100).

Russia, Switzerland, Eastern Europe

Russia: (Population 146 M, rank 9, growth 0%. Not free: 20 of 100. Area 17 M km^2, rank 1)

2 March 2021. Mikhail Gorbachev, Russian and former Soviet politician, the eighth and last leader of the Soviet Union, the General Secretary of the Communist Party of the Soviet Union from 1985 until 1991, Nobel Peace Prize, President of the International Non-Governmental Foundation for Socioeconomic and Political Studies, celebrates his 90th birthday – people wish him Happy Birthday, and remember his extraordinary role in improving the freedom in Russia and many countries around Russia.

4 March 2021. Vladimir Putin held a meeting with the participants in the nationwide mutual assistance campaign We Are Together: …I would like to congratulate you on a whole year of your joint work in this wonderful, noble and highly appreciated field of supporting those who badly need a helping hand.

….It was a drive that united people with very different views – politics no longer matter here – different ages and professions.

….This work is one of the most effective and vibrant ways of self-realization, of self-expression, and self-affirmation in the best sense of the word. It is great that you have reinvented yourself this way.

Note: People congratulate Russia on this success, and kindly ask President Putin to extend this excellent idea of We Are Together to all countries.

Switzerland: (Population 8.4 M, rank 99, growth 0.9%. Free: 96 of 100).

The Swiss firm Debiopharm has signed a €900 M deal with the German big pharma Merck to treat head and neck cancer. In exchange for €188 M upfront and up to €710 M in milestone payments, Debiopharm has granted Merck a global license to develop the phase III-stage compound xevinapant, which makes cancer cells more vulnerable to traditional treatments.

Reports: The drug ponesinod has been approved by the FDA for the treatment of relapsing multiple sclerosis. The drug was added to Janssen's pipeline, when the big pharma acquired the Swiss company Actelion for $30 B in 2017.

Austria: (Population 8.7 M, rank 98, growth 0.3%. Free: 95 of 100).

Poland: (Population 38.1 M, rank 37, decrease 0.1%. Free: 89 of 100).

2 March 2021. Xinhua: Chinese President Xi Jinping said on Monday, 1 March, night that China is willing to provide COVID-19 vaccines within its capabilities to Poland, in accordance with the European country's demand. Xi made the remarks in a phone conversation with Polish President Andrzej Duda.

Pointing out that Poland is a major country in Central and Eastern Europe as well as China's comprehensive strategic partner in Europe, Xi said that China has always attached great importance to the development of China-Poland relations.

Since the outbreak of COVID-19, China and Poland have been looking out for and helping each other, with the two sides engaging in cooperation in pandemic prevention and control as well as resumption of work and production, which opened a new chapter of their friendship, he said.

In the current situation, China and Poland should strengthen strategic communication, deepen pragmatic cooperation, and jointly address various risks and challenges, Xi said.

China is willing to work with Poland to facilitate a stable and sustainable development of bilateral ties in the new year, he added.

Xi said that China is willing to continue enhancing exchanges of experience in joint pandemic prevention and control with the Polish side, and in the meantime restoring mutual visits between their peoples in a safe and orderly manner.

During the pandemic, the number and load of China-Europe freight train trips traveling to and from China and Poland have hit a record high, which reflected the high interdependence between the supply chains and industrial chains in China, Poland, the wider European Union (EU), and demonstrated a huge potential for economic and trade cooperation between the two sides, he said.

China is going to push for more imports of quality agricultural and food products from Poland through establishing relevant mechanisms under the cooperation framework of China-Central and

Eastern European countries (CEEC), Xi said, adding that the completion of negotiations of the China-EU investment agreement will open up broader space for China-Poland cooperation.

Xi said that at the recent China-CEEC Summit successfully convened via video link, he, along with CEEC leaders, reviewed the journey of China-CEEC cooperation, thoroughly summarized development experience, jointly looked ahead to development prospects, reached broad consensus, and made important planning and guidance for cooperation mechanism.

He added that China is willing to work together with the Polish side, and takes the summit as a new starting point to push for greater outcomes for the China-CEEC cooperation and China-EU relations.

Duda said Xi's state visit to Poland in 2016 has effectively promoted the development of Poland-China relations. Not long ago, President Xi successfully hosted the China-CEEC Summit via video link, which is of great importance to promoting cooperation between the two sides and helping CEEC achieve economic recovery after the pandemic. Poland highly appreciates Xi's commitment to making China's COVID-19 vaccine as a global public good, and his willingness to carry out vaccine cooperation with CEEC, which shows China is playing the role of a responsible major country under the leadership of President Xi, Duda said.

He added that Poland is willing to strengthen anti-pandemic cooperation with China, noting that China-Europe freight train service has played an important role in fighting the pandemic.

Duda expressed the hope that the two sides will continue to maintain personnel exchanges and cooperation in various fields and promote the balanced growth of bilateral trade. Poland stands ready to make contributions to the cooperation between CEEC and China, he added.

Duda said he looks forward to visiting China again after the pandemic, and is willing to maintain close and friendly exchanges with Xi to jointly lift Poland-China relations to a new level.

Note: People are glad to see this cooperation, and kindly ask the two countries to focus on peace, freedom, good health, good education, good jobs, good science & technology, harmony and prosperity for all.

Croatia: (Population 4.1 M, rank 129, decrease 0.6%. Free: 87 of 100).

Finland: (Population 5.5 M, rank 116, growth 0.4%. Free: 100 of 100).

As Covid-19 variants sweep the world, the rush is on for big developers to produce vaccines better able to tackle them. The Finnish firm Valo Therapeutics is working on a time-saving alternative: augmenting current vaccines with clip-on peptides.

Romania (Population: 19.6 M, rank 59, decrease 0.5%. Free: 84 of 100)

Moldova: (Population: 4 M, rank 132, decrease 0.2%. Partly Free: 62 of 100).

Operator of Giurgiulesti International Free Port has been a client of the EBRD since the port's inception.

EBRD seeks to safeguard operations of Moldova's Giurgiulesti port, country's only international port, which serves trade with over 50 countries.

Belarus: (Population: 9.4 M, rank 93, decrease 0.1%. Not Free: 20 of 100).

Bulgaria: (Population: 7 M, rank 105, decrease 0.7%. Free: 80 of 100).

Slovenia: (Population: 2 M, rank 148, growth 0.1%. Free: 92 of 100).

Slovakia: (Population: 5.4 M, rank 117, growth 0.1%. Free: 89 of 100).

Hungary: (Population: 9.7 M, rank 91, decrease 0.3%. Free: 76 of 100)

Reports: Hungary has given an emergency authorization to a Covid-19 vaccine developed by the Chinese company CanSino Biologics. This is the second Chinese vaccine to be approved by the

European country, following an initial approval for a candidate developed by Sinopharm.

Ukraine: (Population: 44.2 M, rank 32, decrease 0.5%. Partly free: 61 of 100).

Latvia: (Population: 1.9 M, rank 150, decrease 1.1%. Free: 87 of 100).

Lithuania: (Population: 2.8 M, rank 141, decrease 0.6%. Free: 91 of 100).

Estonia: (Population: 1.3 M, rank 155, decrease 0.2%. Free: 94 of 100).

Serbia: (including Kosovo: Population: 8.7 M, rank 97, decrease 0.3%. Free: 76 of 100.
Kosovo (Disputed: recognized by 110 countries, and not recognized by Serbia, Russia, and others) Population: 1.8 M, Partly free: 52 of 100).

Bosnia and Herzegovina: (Population: 3.5 M, rank 135, decrease 0.3%. Partly free: 55 of 100).

Turkey: (Population 83.7 M, rank 19, growth 1.2%. Partly free: 38 of 100).
8 March 2021. UK Prime Minster Boris Johnson spoke to Turkish President Recep Tayyip Erdoğan this afternoon.
10 March 2021. The Russian President Vladimir Putin and President of the Republic of Turkey Recep Tayyip Erdogan took part in a videoconference ceremony to launch the construction of the third unit of the Akkuyu Nuclear Power Plant in the Mersin Province of Turkey.
Note: All people appreciate this important collaboration, and kindly ask these countries for a strong focus on peace, disarmament, freedom, good health, good education, harmony and prosperity for all.
Report: Turkey's interest rate currently stands at 19%, which has attracted foreign investors to park their cash in the currency. The

lira was at one point the best-performing emerging market currency of 2021, having recovered almost a fifth from a low against the greenback. Naci Agbal, appointed in November, had been raising interest rates to fight an inflation rate running above 15%, and was fired, creating much instability, because of arbitrary decisions.

Greece: (Population 11.1 M, rank 82, decrease 0.2%. Free: 84 of 100).

Hecate was a protector in Greek mythology.

25 March – all people sent greetings to the Greek people on Greek Independence Day, remembering Greece's significant contribution to the world civilization.

Republic of North Macedonia: (Population 2 M, rank 147, growth 0.1%. Partly Free: 57 of 100).

Albania: (Population 2.9 M, rank 139, growth 0.1%. Partly free: 68 of 100).

Cyprus: (Population 1.1 M, rank 159, growth 0.8%. Free: 94 of 100.

Kazakhstan (Population 18.2 M, rank 64, growth 1.2%. Not free: 22 of 100. Area 2.72 M km^2, rank 9.).

Armenia: (Population 2.9 M, rank 138, growth 0.2%. Partly free: 45 of 100).

Azerbaijan: (Population 9.8 M, rank 90, growth 1.1%. Not free 14 of 100).

Uzbekistan: (Population 31.9 M, rank 44, growth 1.5%. Not free: 3 of 100).

Kyrgyzstan (Population 6 M, rank 112, growth 1.5%. Partly free, 37 of 100).

Tajikistan: (Population 8.9 M, rank 96, growth 2.1%. Not free, 11 of 100).

Turkmenistan: (Population 5.7 M, rank 113, growth 1.7%. Not free, 4 of 100).

UK, Cambridge, a bas-relief on the eastern wall of the western building of the Old Court (1451) of Queens' College (1448), University of Cambridge, 60 m east of the Mathematical Bridge (1749).

United Kingdom, Canada, South America

United Kingdom: (Population: 66.1 M, rank 21, growth 0.6%. Free: 95 of 100).

Reports: The UK company Oxular has closed a €31.4 M funding round led by the Dutch venture capital firm Forbion. Oxular will use part of the money to fund the clinical development of a treatment for the eye condition diabetic macular edema. Oxular's treatments are designed to last for up to a year after injection into the eye, and allow the selective targeting of tissues involved in eye disease.

12 March 2021. Reports: UK schools, colleges and universities can now apply for funding for opportunities targeted at disadvantaged students. Schools, colleges and universities can now apply for funding from today (Friday 12 March) to allow students to study and work across the globe as part of the new Turing Scheme. The programme, backed by £110 M, replaces the Erasmus+ scheme in the UK and will fund 35,000 global exchanges from September 2021, including university study, school exchanges, and industry work placements. Unlike Erasmus+, which is EU-focused, the Turing Scheme is a truly global programme and every country in the world is eligible to partner with UK universities, schools and colleges.

Prime Minister, Boris Johnson said:

The Turing Scheme is a truly global programme with every country in the world eligible to partner with UK universities, schools and colleges.

It is also levelling up in action, as the scheme seeks to help students of all income groups from across the country experience fantastic education opportunities in any country they choose.

Note: All people are glad to see this initiative, and hope to see extensions to peace, no arms, freedom, good health, harmony and prosperity for all.

Reports: Scientists at The University of Manchester have developed a technique to identify Parkinson's based on compounds found on the surface of skin.

Reports: The Oxford-based startup Vaccitech is working on the phase I/II development of a therapeutic vaccine for prostate cancer, and candidates against human papillomavirus and chronic hepatitis B infections. The company, which played a role in the development of the AstraZeneca/Oxford Covid-19 vaccine, also has vaccines in the works for other conditions including MERS and herpes zoster.

20 March 2021. Prime Minister Boris Johnson held a video call with four British National (Overseas) families from Hong Kong, who have come to the UK following the imposition of the National Security Law, and the UK's offer of a pathway to British citizenship for BN(O) status holders. BN(O) status holders and their dependents have been able to formally apply for the visa since the end of January, and in that time we have received 27,000 applications from those wishing to come and pursue a new life in the UK.

Since February, Hong Kong BN(O) status holders with certain biometric passports have been able to apply for their visa using a smartphone app to scan their passport rather than visiting a visa center – the first time non-EEA passport holders have been able to use this technology to apply, a further step in the UK's digitization of our immigration system.

Reports: The UK startup Dunad Therapeutics's drugs degrade harmful proteins, and are designed to stand out from others in the protein degradation field, by being taken orally and being able to reach the central nervous system.

31 March 2021. Prime Minister Boris Johnson's joint article with other world leaders.

No government can address the threat of pandemics alone – we must come together

The Covid-19 pandemic is the biggest challenge to the global community since the 1940s.

At that time, following the devastation of two world wars, political leaders came together to forge the multilateral system. The aims were clear – to bring countries together, to dispel the temptations of isolationism and nationalism and to address the challenges that could only be achieved together in the spirit of solidarity and co-operation, namely peace, prosperity, health and security.

Today we hold the same hope that, as we fight to overcome the Covid-19 pandemic together, we can build a more robust international health architecture that will protect future generations.

There will be other pandemics and other major health emergencies. No single government or multilateral agency can address this threat alone. The question is not if, but when. Together, we must be better prepared to predict, prevent, detect, assess and effectively respond to pandemics in a highly co-ordinated fashion. The Covid-19 pandemic has been a stark and painful reminder that nobody is safe until everyone is safe.

We are, therefore, committed to ensuring universal and equitable access to safe, efficacious and affordable vaccines, medicines and diagnostics for this and future pandemics.

Immunization is a global public good and we will need to be able to develop, manufacture and deploy vaccines as quickly as possible.

This is why the Access to Covid-19 Tools Accelerator (ACT-A) was set up in order to promote equal access to tests, treatments and vaccines and support health systems across the globe. ACT-A has delivered on many aspects, but equitable access is not achieved yet. There is more we can do to promote global access.

To that end, we believe that nations should work together towards a new international treaty for pandemic preparedness and response. Such a renewed collective commitment would be a milestone in stepping up pandemic preparedness at the highest political level. It would be rooted in the constitution of the World Health Organization, drawing in other relevant organizations key to this endeavor, in support of the principle of health for all.

Existing global health instruments, especially the International Health Regulations, would underpin such a treaty, ensuring a firm and tested foundation on which we can build and improve.

The main goal of this treaty would be to foster an all of government and all of society approach, strengthening national, regional and global capacities and resilience to future pandemics. This includes greatly enhancing international co-operation to improve, for example, alert systems, data-sharing, research and local, regional and global production and distribution of medical and public health counter-measures such as vaccines, medicines, diagnostics and personal protective equipment.

It would also include recognition of a "One Health" approach that connects the health of humans, animals and our planet. And such a treaty should lead to more mutual accountability and shared responsibility, transparency and co-operation within the international system and with its rules and norms.

To achieve this, we will work with heads of state and governments globally, and all stakeholders including civil society and the private sector. We are convinced that it is our responsibility, as leaders of nations and international institutions, to ensure that the world learns the lessons of the Covid-19 pandemic.

At a time when Covid-19 has exploited our weaknesses and divisions, we must seize this opportunity and come together as a global community for peaceful co-operation that extends beyond this crisis. Building our capacities and systems to do this will take time and require a sustained political, financial and societal commitment over many years.

Our solidarity in ensuring that the world is better prepared will be our legacy that protects our children and grandchildren and minimizes the impact of future pandemics on our economies and our societies.

Pandemic preparedness needs global leadership for a global health system fit for this millennium. To make this commitment a reality, we must be guided by solidarity, fairness, transparency, inclusiveness and equity.

Authors:

J. V. Bainimarama, Prime Minister of Fiji

António Luís Santos da Costa, Prime Minister of Portugal

Klaus Iohannis, President of Romania

Boris Johnson, Prime Minister of the United Kingdom

Paul Kagame, President of Rwanda

Uhuru Kenyatta, President of Kenya

Emmanuel Macron, President of France

Angela Merkel, Chancellor of Germany

Charles Michel, President of the European Council

Kyriakos Mitsotakis, Prime Minister of Greece

Moon Jae-in, President of the Republic of Korea

Sebastián Piñera, President of Chile

Carlos Alvarado Quesada, President of Costa Rica

Edi Rama, Prime Minister of Albania

Cyril Ramaphosa, President of South Africa

Keith Rowley, Prime Minister of Trinidad and Tobago

Mark Rutte, Prime Minister of the Netherlands

Kais Saied, President of Tunisia
Macky Sall, President of Senegal
Pedro Sánchez, Prime Minister of Spain
Erna Solberg, Prime Minister of Norway
Aleksandar Vučić, President of Serbia
Joko Widodo, President of Indonesia
Volodymyr Zelensky, President of Ukraine
Dr Tedros Adhanom Ghebreyesus, Director-General of the World Health Organization

Note: All people congratulate these 25 leaders for this excellent article! All people support these ideas, and will work with these leaders to implement them, in order to have good health, peace, no arms, freedom, good education, good jobs, harmony and prosperity for all! There is no doubt whatsoever that we the people will succeed!

Ireland: (Population: 4.7 M, rank 123, growth 0.8%. Free: 96 of 100)

Canada: (Population: 36.6 M, rank 38, growth 0.9%. Free: 99 of 100. Area 9.9 M km^2, rank 2).
23 February 2021. US President Joe Biden and Prime Minister Justin Trudeau held their first bilateral meeting.

Iceland: (Population: 335,000, rank 180, growth 0.8%. Free 97 of 100).

Mexico: (Population: 129.1 M, rank 10, growth 1.3%. Partly Free: 65 of 100. Area 1.96 M km^2, rank 13).

Chile: (Population: 18 M, rank 65, growth 0.8%. Free 94 of 100).

Colombia: (Population: 49 M, rank 29, growth 0.8%. Partly free 64 of 100).

Argentina: (Population: 44.2 M, rank 31, growth, 1%. Free: 82 of 100. Area 2.78 M km^2, rank 8.).

Brazil (Population: 209.2 M, rank 6, growth 0.8%. Free, 79 of 100. Area 8.5 M km^2, rank 5).

Ecuador: (Population: 17.3 M, rank 67, growth 1.7%. Partly free: 57 of 100)

Peru: (Population: 32.1 M, rank 43, growth 1.2%. Free: 72 of 100)

Cuba: (Population: 11.4 M, rank 81, growth 0.1%. Not free, 15 of 100).

Bolivia: (Population: 11.5 M, rank 80, growth 1.5%. Partly free 68 of 100).

Paraguay: (Population: 6.8 M, rank 107, growth 1.3%. Partly free 64 of 100).

Panama: (Population: 4.1 M, rank 131, growth 1.6%. Free: 83 of 100).

Venezuela: (Population: 32 M, rank 43, growth 1.3%. Not free: 30 of 100).

Guyana: (Population 777K, (rank 165, growth 0.6%). Free: 74 of 100).

Trinidad and Tobago: (Population 1.3 M, (rank 153, growth 0.3%). Free: 81 of 100).

Nicaragua: (Population 6.2 M, (rank 110, growth 1.1%). Partly Free: 47 of 100).

El Salvador: (Population 6.3 M (rank 108, growth 0.5%). Free: 70 of 100).

Guatemala: (Population 17.6 M (rank 89, growth 1.93%). Partly Free: 52 of 100).

Costa Rica: (Population 5 M (rank 120, growth 0.96%). Free: 91 of 100).

France, Paris, the north-west part of L'Institut de France (1795, moved in 1805 by Napoléon in this baroque building from 1684) is a revered French cultural society with five académies, the most famous being Académie Français (1635) and. Académie des sciences (1666).

France, Germany, and neighbors

France: (Population 64.9 M, rank 22, growth 0.4%. Free: 90 of 100).

Reports: The French company Step Pharma is working on the clinical testing of a treatment for cancers associated with immune T and B cells. The drug targets a protein called cytidine nucleotide triphosphate, which is required for DNA synthesis and cell division, and blocking the protein could stop cancerous immune T and B cells from multiplying out of control.

Reports: Hommage à Eugène Ionesco (26 Nov 1909 – 28 March 1994, 84.3) - grand dramaturge né en Roumanie et devenu célèbre en France.

30 March 2921. The Russian President Vladimir Putin had talks, via videoconference, with Federal Chancellor of the Federal Republic of Germany Angela Merkel, and President of the French Republic Emmanuel Macron.

The talks focused on the task of consolidating efforts against a common threat, the coronavirus pandemic. In this context, the leaders discussed measures to prevent the further spread of the infection, including the outlook for the registration of the Russian Sputnik V vaccine in the EU, and possible deliveries and joint production of the vaccine in the EU countries.

During an in-depth exchange of views on the situation in Ukraine, the leaders confirmed the lack of alternatives to the 2015 Minsk Package of Measures as the basis for a settlement of the internal conflict in that country. The President of Russia emphasized that it is important that the Kiev authorities implement all the previous agreements reached at the top level, primarily on establishing a direct dialogue with Donetsk and Lugansk and settling the legal aspects of a special status for Donbass. The Russian leader expressed serious concern about the escalation of armed confrontation on the contact line, being provoked by Ukraine, and its refusal to implement the additional measures to strengthen the ceasefire coordinated by the Trilateral Contact Group in July 2020. The leaders' political advisers will continue their joint efforts.

When talking about the developments in Belarus, Vladimir Putin pointed out that foreign interference in the affairs of that sovereign state is unacceptable. The leaders also discussed a settlement in Libya. They noted with satisfaction that the conflicting sides complied with the ceasefire regime, and expressed hope that the establishment of united transitional authorities in the country would become a major step towards an effective political process involving all the main Libyan forces. It was pointed out that the situation in Syria continued stabilizing, and that one of the priority issues was the provision of humanitarian aid to the Syrian people.

The leaders of Russia, Germany and France unambiguously called for the preservation and implementation of the Joint Comprehensive Plan of Action (JCPOA) on Iran's nuclear programme and continued coordination of efforts towards this objective.

They also discussed relations between Russia and the EU. The Russian leader reaffirmed Russia's readiness to restore a normal depoliticized interaction with the EU, provided there is reciprocal interest. Regarding the issue of Alexei Navalny raised by the partners, explanations of the objective circumstances of the case were provided. Overall, the talks were held in a business-like and frank atmosphere. It was agreed to continue working together on all aspects of the current agenda.

Note: People are glad to see that the great powers Russia, France and Germany continue to have useful discussions, to the benefit of their peoples, as well as the peoples of EU, Ukraine, Donbass, Belarus, Libya, Syria, Iran, and all people on Earth – all people want peace, no arms, no conflicts, freedom, good health, good education, good jobs, harmony and prosperity for all. The issue of Alexei Navalny can be easily and quickly solved by having him and his friends immediately moved to temporary house arrest, with daily medical visits for detailed discussions, and with available access to the President of France, the Federal Chancellor of the Federal Republic of Germany, and their medical representatives. After several days of calm, constructive and friendly discussions, all the temporary house arrests will be terminated, and everybody will return to normal and pleasant life. Also, the conflicts in Donbass, Belarus, Libya and Syria can be quickly resolved by eliminating all the arms in the conflict region, and sending plenty of medical personnel, teachers and businessmen to talk to all the people in conflict, find out a reasonable solution for them, and then begin to implement it with economic, medical and educational assistance – in a matter of weeks the conflicts will disappear.

Belgium (Population 11.4 M, rank 80, growth 0.6%. Free: 95 of 100).

European Commission, European Union, EU: 27 EU countries: Austria, Belgium, Bulgaria, Croatia, Republic of Cyprus, Czech Republic, Denmark, Estonia, Finland, France, Germany, Greece, Hungary, Ireland, Italy, Latvia, Lithuania, Luxembourg, Malta, Netherlands, Poland, Portugal, Romania, Slovakia, Slovenia, Spain, and Sweden.

Reports: The bureaucracy, regulations and related abuses in EU are increasing, to the detriment of the people.

25 March 2021. Reports: EU leaders conflicted over vaccine distribution at a marathon virtual summit on Thursday, 25 March, and failed to settle a dispute about supply of the jabs among member states. Austrian Chancellor Sebastian Kurz criticized the allocation of shots, demanding additional supplies to Vienna, while some brought up the vaccine share of poorer Eastern European states. The countries failed to come to an agreement.

The **European Council** is made up of the heads of state or government of all EU countries, the European Council President, and the European Commission President.

22 March 2021. Vladimir Putin had a telephone conversation with President of the European Council Charles Michel.

Considering the upcoming discussion of Russia-EU relations at the meeting on March 25–26, Charles Michel touched on several issues related to the current state and prospects of the dialogue between Moscow and Brussels.

Vladimir Putin assessed the unsatisfactory state of Russian-EU ties that has resulted from nonconstructive and sometimes a confrontational course of the partners. Russia reaffirmed its readiness to restore a normal depoliticized format of interaction with the European Union, if real interest from the other side is shown.

Issues related to countering the coronavirus pandemic, in particular, ways to use the Russian vaccine, Sputnik V, the political settlement process in Ukraine, developments in Belarus and several other topical matters were also discussed.

NATO 29 member states: Albania, Belgium, Bulgaria, Canada, Croatia, Czech Republic, Denmark, Estonia, France, Germany, Greece, Hungary, Iceland, Italy, Latvia, Lithuania, Luxembourg, Montenegro, Netherlands, Norway, Poland, Portugal, Romania, Slovakia, Slovenia, Spain, Turkey, United Kingdom, and United States

NATO was created in 1949 with 12 states, and now includes 29 countries. The aggregate war-related expenses of its members exceed 70% of the world's total war-related spending.

Germany: (Population 82.1 M, rank 16, growth 0.2%. Free: 95 of 100).

Reports: On Tuesday, 23 March, Chancellor Angela Merkel called the dominant U.K. variant of the coronavirus a "new pandemic", and outlined tighter shutdown measures in Germany. The Netherlands and France also extended lockdowns and imposed new travel and business curbs.

Reports: Germany is by far the biggest market for food and beverages in the European Union. The food processing industry represents the third-largest industry in Germany. In 2019, Germany produced an estimated USD 221.7 billions of processed food and drinks. When meeting EU standards, the following products have good sales potential on the German market: nuts, fish and seafood products, highly processed ingredients, dried fruits, sweet potatoes, bakery products, organic products, and pulses.

Reports: In a fresh blow to AstraZeneca's COVID-19 vaccine, Germany says it will halt its use for people under 60 starting Wednesday, 31 March. The move, endorsed by regional health ministers and announced by Chancellor Angela Merkel, comes after new cases of blood clots associated with the vaccine. The clots mainly occur in those under 60. "These are findings that we cannot ignore," Merkel said late Tuesday, according to Bloomberg. "We all know that vaccination is the most important tool against the coronavirus - that we have different vaccines at our disposal is our good fortune." The Paul Ehrlich Institute reported that as of March 29, a total of 31 cases of blood clots have been reported out of 2.7

M AstraZeneca vaccine doses administered in Germany. The vaccine was already suspended in regions of Germany yesterday.

Norway (Population 5.3 M, rank 118, growth 1%. Free: 100 of 100).

Sweden (Population 9.9 M, rank 89, growth 0.7%. Free: 100 of 100).
Reports: The drug Pepaxto has been granted accelerated approval by the FDA for the treatment of heavily drug-resistant blood cancer. The drug, developed by the Swedish company Oncopeptides, consists of a peptide carrying an anticancer drug, and is expected to become available in the US within the next two weeks.

The Netherlands (Population 17 M, rank 67, growth 0.3%. Free: 99 of 100).
On 1 January, Amsterdam surpassed London as Europe's largest share trading center.
The Dutch firm Leyden Labs will develop a nasal spray that protects against a variety of respiratory infections by viruses, including coronaviruses and influenza viruses.

Czech Republic (Population 10.6 M, rank 87, growth 0.1%. Free: 94 of 100).

Denmark (Population 5.7 M, rank 114, growth 0.4%. Free: 97 of 100. Area (including Greenland) 2.22 M km^2, rank 12 but not official).

Luxembourg (Population 583 K, rank 169, growth 1.3%. Free: 98 of 100).
10 March 2021. The Russian President Vladimir Putin had a telephone conversation with Prime Minister of the Grand Duchy of Luxembourg, Xavier Bettel, at the initiative of the Luxembourg party. Vladimir Putin and Xavier Bettel discussed topical issues on the bilateral agenda, noting the traditionally friendly and constructive nature of Russia-Luxembourg cooperation, including in the context of the 130th anniversary of the establishment of diplomatic relations, marked just recently. Both sides reaffirmed

their mutual striving to expand political contacts, trade and economic, and cultural and humanitarian ties.

Special attention was paid to cooperation in the area of countering the spread of the coronavirus infection, including possible prospects for supplying Russia's Sputnik V vaccine to Luxembourg.

Vladimir Putin and Xavier Bettel also touched upon the current status of the dialogue between Russia and the European Union.

Spain: (Population 46.3 M, rank 30, growth 0%. Free: 94 of 100).

Reports: COVID-19 had an unexpected effect on the Spanish food distribution sector. Spanish consumers spent $3.7 B more at supermarkets compared to 2019. Changing consumer patterns in 2020 disrupted the long-historic ranking of the top three food retailers in Spain (Mercadona, Carrefour, and DIA). Retailer Lidl replaced DIA as the new third ranking retailer. Flooded with an unprecedented number of customers in this new post-COVID scenario, supermarkets in Spain are now fighting to obtain a larger share of customers with some chains starting a price competition that is expected to continue in 2021.

Portugal: (Population 10.3 M, rank 88, decrease 0.4%. Free: 97 of 100).

Reports: Similar to other consumers around the world, consumers in Portugal continue to adapt their lives and habits to the situation under the COVID-19 pandemic. Technological advances, changing consumer demographics and navigating this new environment will continue to impact Portuguese consumer behavior in the short and medium term. Portuguese consumers remain the greatest promotional consumers in Europe, but taste is also a very influential factor when choosing food products. Many Portuguese have traveled or have strong ties to the United States and appreciate U.S. food products and culture.

Liechtenstein: (Population: 38,000, rank 215, growth 0.7%, Free: 91 of 100)

Andorra: (Population: 77,100, rank 203, growth 0.18%, Free: 94 of 100)

India, Pakistan, Australia, and neighbors

India (Population: 1.3 B, rank 2nd, growth 1.1%. Free: 77 of 100. Area 3.28 M km^2, rank 7).

Reports: India wants to ban cryptos, giving holders of the virtual assets up to six months to liquidate. The bill, one of the world's strictest policies against cryptocurrencies, would criminalize everything from possession, issuance and mining to trading and transferring crypto assets. It's not the first nation to take action against Bitcoin, with similar bans or restrictions seen in countries like China, Pakistan, Russia, Bolivia, North Macedonia and Morocco. There are concerns that Bitcoin's decentralized system will make it more complicated for central banks to create their own CBDCs (central bank digital currencies), as well as worries that cryptos are being used to finance illicit activities.

Indonesia: (Population: 263.9 M, rank 4, growth 1.1%. Partly free: 65 of 100. Area 1.91 M km^2, rank 14.).

Australia: (Population: 24.4 M, rank 53, growth 1.3%. Free: 98 of 100. Area 7.69 M km^2, rank 6).

New Zealand: (Population 4.7 M, rank 125, growth 1%. Free: 98 of 100.

Pakistan: (Population 212 M, rank 5, growth 2%. Partly free: 43 of 100).

Philippines: (Population 104.9 M, rank 13, growth 1.5%. Partly free 63 of 100).

Singapore: (Population 5.7 M, rank 115, growth 1.5%. Partly free 51 of 100).

Important World Congress: the 7th World Congress of Smart Materials 2022 (WCSM2022)-Singapore, which will be held in Singapore from June 15-17, 2022.

The <u>EAS</u> (East Asia Summit) currently comprises 18 countries: 10 <u>ASEAN</u> (Association of South-East Asian Nations) members (Brunei Darussalam, Cambodia, Indonesia, Laos, Malaysia, Myanmar, the Philippines, Singapore, Thailand and Vietnam), and eight dialogue partners: Russia (joined the EAS in 2010), the United States, Japan, South Korea, India, China, Australia and New Zealand.

<u>APEC</u> (Asia-Pacific Economic Cooperation: 21 members: Singapore, China, USA, Vietnam, Australia, Japan, Indonesia, Russia, Philippines, Malaysia, Hong Kong, Thailand, Chile, Canada, New Zealand, South Korea, Peru, Mexico, Brunei, Papua New Guinea, Chinese Taipei)

Thailand: (Population 69 M, rank 20, growth 0.3%. Not free 32 of 100).

Myanmar (Burma), Population 53.3 M, rank 26, growth 0.9%. Not free 32 of 100.

Bangladesh (Population 164.6 M, rank 8, growth 1.1%. Partly free 47 of 100).

Sri Lanka (Population 20.8 M, rank 58, growth 0.4%. Partly free 56 of 100).

Malaysia (Population 31.6 M, rank 45, growth 1.34%. Partly free 44 of 100).

Brunei: (Population 428,000, rank 176, growth 1.3%. Not free 29 of 100).

Vanuatu: (Population 276,000, rank 185, growth 2.2%. Free 80 of 100)

Tonga: (Population 108,000, rank 195, growth 0.8%. Free 74 of 100

Papua New Guinea: (Population 8.2 M, rank 101, growth 2.1%, Partly Free 64 of 100).

Italy, Middle East, Africa

Italy: (Population 59.3 M, rank 23, decrease 0.1%. Free: 89 of 100).

4 March 2021. The UK Prime Minister Boris Johnson spoke to Italian Prime Minister Mario Draghi this afternoon.

Vatican: (Population 792, rank 233 (last), decrease 1.1%).

San Marino: (Population 33,400, rank 218, growth 0.6%. Free 97 of 100)

Malta (Population 431,000, rank 175, growth 0.3%. Free, 96 of 100).

Jordan (Population 9.7 M, rank 92, growth 2.6%. Partly free, 37 of 100).

Lebanon: (Population: 6 M, rank 111, growth 1.3%. Partly free: 44 of 100).

United Arab Emirates (UAE) (Population: 9.4 M, rank 94, growth 1.4%. Not free, 20 of 100. Capital: Abu Dhabi. Big city: Dubai).

Saudi Arabia (Population 32.9 M, rank 41, growth 2.1%. Not free: 10 of 100. Area 2.149 M km^2, rank 12.).

8 March 2021. Reports: A key Saudi oil site (the Ras Tanura export terminal) came under attack by missiles and bomb-laden drones. Iranian-backed Houthi rebels in Yemen claimed responsibility for the assault on the Ras Tanura export terminal, which is capable of exporting about 6.5 M barrels a day (nearly 7% of global demand).

Yemen (Population 28.2 M, rank 50, growth 2.4%. Not free: 14 of 100).

Reports: Yemen has been devastated by a six-year civil war, in which more than 110,000 people are believed to have died.

Note: People express condolences to the families of the victims, and ask for a prompt solution, which is an intense demilitarization of Yemen, all arms prohibited, major increase of medical personnel (to visit and register all people), businesses, teachers and police, national and local calm and friendly elections every year, national referenda every 3 months, heavy UN civilian assistance.

Iraq (Population 38.2 M, rank 36, growth 2.9%. Not free: 27 of 100).

Iran: (Population 81.1 M, rank 18, growth 1.1%. Not free: 17 of 100).

Israel: (Population 8.3 M, rank 100, growth 1.6%. Free: 80 of 100).

Palestine: (Population 4.9 M (rank 121, grows 2.7%). Not free: 28 of 100).

Egypt (Population 97.5 M (rank 14, grows 1.9%). Not free, 26 of 100).

24 March 2021. Reports: Tugs and diggers have so far failed to dislodge the Ever Given, a massive container ship stuck in the Suez Canal, after losing the ability to steer amid high winds and a dust storm. Some shipping firms will be forced to re-route vessels around the southern tip of Africa, which would add roughly a week to the journey. About 12% of global trade and roughly 30% of the world's shipping container volume transit through the Suez Canal, making it one of the world's most important waterways. A rough estimate shows the blockage is costing about $400 M/hour, based on calculations from Lloyd's List.

26 March 2021. People transmit sincere condolences to the families of the victims, to the people of Egypt, and to the President of the Arab Republic of Egypt, Abdel Fattah el-Sisi, over the tragic consequences of the train crash in Sohag governorate. Again, sincere sympathy and support to the victims' families and friends, and wishes of speedy recovery for the injured.

Note: Help is necessary to improve the maintenance and security of the Suez Canal, railroads, and related areas.

League of Arab States (LAS) (22 countries: Algeria, Bahrein, Comoros, Djibouti, Egypt, Iraq, Jordan, Kuwait, Lebanon, Libya, Mauritania, Morocco, Oman, Palestine, Qatar, Saudi Arabia, Somalia, Sudan, Syria, Tunisia, United Arab Emirates and Yemen).

Qatar: (Population 2.6 M (rank 142, grows 2.7%). Not free: 26 of 100).

Kuwait: (Population 4.1 M (rank 130, grows 2.1%). Partly free: 36 of 100).

Oman: (Population 4.6 M (rank 127, grows 4.8%). Not free: 25 of 100)

Bahrain: (Population 1.5 M (rank 152, grows 4.7%). Not free: 12 of 100).

Syria: (Population 18.2 M (rank 63, decrease 0.9%). Not free: 0 of 100).

Kenya: (Population 49.7 M (rank 28, growth 2.6%. Partly free, 51 of 100).

Libya: (Population 6.3 M, rank 109, growth 1.3%. Not free: 13 of 100).

Algeria: (Population 41.3 M, rank 34, growth 1.8%. Partly Free 35 of 100. Area 2.38 M km^2, rank 10.)

Tunisia: (Population 11.5 M, rank 78, growth 1.1%. Free: 78 of 100).

Morocco: (Population 35.7 M, rank 39, growth 1.3%. Partly free: 41 of 100).

South Africa: (Population 56.7 M, rank 25, growth 1.3%. Free, 78 of 100).

Zimbabwe: (Population 16.5 M, rank 70, growth 2.4%. Partly Free, 32 of 100).

Sudan (Population 40.5 M, rank 35, growth 2.4%. Not Free: 6 of 100).

South Sudan (Population 12.5 M, rank 76, growth 2.8%. Not Free: 4 of 100)

Guinea: (Population 12.7 M, rank 75, growth 2.6%. Partly Free, 41 of 100).

Djibouti (Population 957,000, rank 160, growth 1.6%. Not Free: 26 of 100).

Somalia: (Population 14.7 M, rank 74, growth 3%. Not free: 5 of 100).

Niger (Population 21.4 M, rank 57, growth 3.9%. Partly free: 49 of 100).

Nigeria (Population 206 M, rank 7, growth 2.6%. Partly free: 50 of 100).

Cameroon (Population 24 M, rank 55, growth 2.6%. Not free: 24 of 100).

Sierra Leone: (Population 7.5 M (rank 103, grows 2.2%). Partly free: 66 of 100)

Chad: (Population 15 M (rank 73, grows 3.1%). Not free: 18 of 100).

The Gambia: (Population 2.1 M (rank 146, grows 3%). Not free: 20 of 100).

Malawi: (Population 18.6 M (rank 61, grows 2.9%). Partly free: 63 of 100).

Rwanda: (Population 12.2 M (rank 77, grows 2.4%). Not free: 24 of 100).

Burkina Faso: (Population 19.1 M (rank 60, grows 2.9%). Partly free: 63 of 100).

Central African Republic: (Population 4.6 M (rank 126, grows 1.4%). Not free: 10 of 100).

Senegal: (Population 15.8 M (rank 72, grows 2.8%). Free: 78 of 100).

Gabon: (Population 2 M (rank 149, grows 2.3%). Partly Free: 32 of 100).

Madagascar: (Population 25.5 M (rank 51, grows 2.7%). Partly Free: 56 of 100).

Democratic Republic of the Congo: (Population 81.3 M (rank 17, grows 3.3%). Not Free: 19 of 100. Area 2.34 M km^2, rank 11).

Angola: (Population 29.7 M (rank 46, grows 3.4%). Not Free: 24 of 100).

Zambia: (Population 17 M (rank 66, grows 3%). Partly Free: 56 of 100).

United Republic of Tanzania: (Population 57 M (rank 24, grows 3.1%). Partly Free: 58 of 100).

Ethiopia: (Population 105 M (rank 12, grows 2.5%). Not Free: 12 of 100).

Uganda: (Population 42.8 M (rank 33, grows 3.3%). Partly Free: 35 of 100).

Mozambique: (Population 30.3 M (rank 46, grows 2.9%). Partly Free: 53 of 100).

Namibia: (Population 2.5 M (rank 143, grows 1.9%). Free: 77 of 100).

Mauritius: (Population 1.2 M (rank 157, growth 0.8%). Free: 89 of 100).

Equatorial Guinea: (Population 1.35 M (rank 154, growth 3.6%). Not Free: 8 of 100).

Ghana: (Population 28.8 M (rank 48, growth 2.22%). Free: 83 of 100).

Côte d'Ivoire: (Population 25.7 M (rank 106, growth 2.58%). Partly Free: 51 of 100).

A south-west view of Rome from Altare della Patria: Theatrum Marcelli (the Theatre of Marcellus (Marcus Claudius Marcellus, 42 BC – 23 BC, Emperor Augustus' nephew), 13 BC, left back).

Medical

Tetanus shot is suggested every 10 years.

Led by engineers at George Washington University and Northwestern University, researchers have developed a new class of medical instruments to improve the diagnoses and treatments of cardiac diseases. They applied stretchable matrices of electrode sensors and actuators, along with temperature and pressure sensors, to a balloon catheter system for minimally invasive surgeries.

Marijuana is dangerous for people.

Understanding tumor status and its environment is critical to the success of oncology trials. There are new tools that better capture a snapshot of the tumor microenvironment (TME) as well as its hot and cold status.

Consciousness is related to the material brain and its neurons.

COVID-19 can be diagnosed in 55 minutes or less with the help of programmed magnetic nanobeads and a diagnostic tool that plugs into an off-the-shelf cell phone. Engineers have developed a stamp-sized microfluidic chip that measures the concentration of SARS-CoV-2 nucleocapsid (N) protein in blood serum from a standard finger prick.

The origin of life is at infinite.

The biologists cannot create life from scratch in the laboratory.

Protein AEG12 strongly inhibits the family of viruses that cause yellow fever, dengue, West Nile, and Zika.

Specialists want to transform cancer pathology with AI.

An antibiotic sensitivity test can find out which antibiotic will be most effective in treating an infection.

33% of COVID-19 patients with factor V activity well above the reference range had either deep vein thrombosis or a pulmonary embolism.

A wearable microgrid from the University of California San Diego harvests and stores energy from the body to keep the electronics going.

Pets bring many more negative issues than benefits.

Remote patient monitoring and chronic care management increase the medical effectiveness.

Reports: BridgeBio Pharma is due to present Phase 2 data on encaleret on Type 1 autosomal dominant hypocalcemia at Endocrine Society's 2021 Annual Meeting.

Rhythm Pharmaceuticals and Spruce Biosciences will have the latest set of data likely to be presented at a virtual 3-day event. Insulet Corporation will host an investor webcast focused on the Omnipod 5 pivotal trial data for adults and adolescents presented at ENDO 2021.

Late Monday, 22 March, the Data and Safety Monitoring Board (DSMB) notified NIAID, BARDA, and AstraZeneca that it was concerned by information released by AstraZeneca on initial data from its COVID-19 vaccine clinical trial.

AstraZeneca may have provided the U.S. outdated information that gave an "incomplete" view about the efficacy of its vaccine, according to the U.S. Data Safety and Monitoring Board. "The DSMB expressed concern that AstraZeneca may have included outdated information from that trial, which may have provided an incomplete view of the efficacy data. We urge the company to work with the DSMB to review the efficacy data and ensure the most accurate, up-to-date efficacy data be made public as quickly as possible," the National Institute for Allergy and Infectious Diseases, headed by Dr Anthony Fauci, said in a statement.

A new study, a pre-proof of which was published in the American Journal of Obstetrics & Gynecology, found the mRNA COVID-19 vaccines made by Pfizer and Moderna are safe and effective for pregnant women. Pfizer also started clinical trials of its COVID-19 vaccine on healthy children aged 6 months to 11. They will begin receiving a 10 micrograms dose of the vaccine before progressively moving to higher doses, though the option for 3 micrograms doses is also available (vaccines for adults require two shots that contain 30 micrograms per dose).

Reports: Age-related muscle loss, called sarcopenia, is a natural part of getting older. But after an injury, illness, or any prolonged period of inactivity, muscle loss can occur faster, leading to muscle atrophy. The consequences are greater weakness, poor balance, and even frailty.

There has been a wave of approvals of Covid-19 vaccines based on viral vectors, called adenoviruses, this year. There are big challenges going forward, such as overcoming immunity to the viral vector.

With traditional tumor biopsies proving invasive or inaccessible, researchers are turning towards plasma biospecimens for insights.

Parkinson's disease is an incurable neurodegenerative disease affecting millions around the world. There are biotechs developing ways to turn the immune system against toxic proteins potentially underlying the condition.

AstraZeneca reported a phase III efficacy of 76% for its Covid-19 vaccine. This announcement came days after the big pharma received a rebuke from US health officials, who raised concerns that this week's earlier figure of 79% was out of date.

T cells recognize recent SARS-CoV-2 variants - NIH research suggests protective effects of vaccination remain intact.

Scientists developed a SARS-CoV-2 vaccine by adding a key coronavirus gene to the measles vaccine.

A fungus called *Debaryomyces hansenii* impaired gut wound healing in mice, and was also found in damaged gut tissue in people with Crohn's disease.

Turning off a particular gene prevented or alleviated chronic pain in mice. The results could lead to an alternative to opioids for treating chronic pain.

Preventive treatment reduces diabetic retinopathy complications - NIH-funded study shows early eye injections reduce vision-threatening complications; effect on vision similar to standard treatment.

Reports: Regeneron's Eylea reduces vision loss by 68% after two years in diabetic retinopathy.

Nitrogen dioxide, an air pollutant emitted by fossil fuel-powered cars and gas-burning stoves is bad for our health. Long-term exposure to NO_2 has been linked to increased heart disease, respiratory diseases such as asthma, and infections. Nitrogen dioxide is odorless and invisible.

64

Mathematics, Science, Technology, AI, Space

Cybersecurity for all: all computers will have a place for the user's card – the user's card will have the information about the user, will be registered (for a small fee) with the local cyber-police (which will be connected to the world cyber-police), and the user's card will appear on all the computers contacted by that user and on user's e-mails. If something unfriendly comes from a computer, it's user card number will be given to the cyber-police, who will immediately contact the user.

Chips are a hot topic leading into an AMD event on March 3 to introduce the newest addition to the Radeon RX family of high-performance graphic cards. The new model is expected to be the Radeon RX 6700 XT, aimed to compete with Nvidia's mid-range Ampere-based graphics cards

When SpaceX's Crew Dragon capsule splashed down off the Florida coast in August 2020, following its first crewed mission, the two astronauts inside could not exit the capsule immediately. Technicians outside had to confirm there were no airborne vapors from hydrazine, a highly toxic fuel used by the vehicle's hypergolic thrusters.

18 November 2020. SoloHI imager captured rare shot of Venus, Earth (251 M km), Mars, and Uranus - the European Space Agency's (ESA) and NASA's Solar Orbiter Heliospheric Imager (SoloHI) recorded a beautiful image showing three of the four inner rocky planets, as well as the ice giant Uranus which was more than 2.7 billions of kilometers from the orbiter, more than 10 times farther than Venus, Earth and Mars.

Hominis is the first surgical robot with arms, designed to replicate the motions and capabilities of a surgeon's arms, with shoulder, elbow, and wrist joints, allowing the robot to access and reach through areas not possible with other robots.

Engineers at UC San Diego have created a four-legged soft robot that requires no electronics to walk — just a constant source of pressurized air.

Important World Congress: the 7th World Congress of Smart Materials 2022 (WCSM2022)-Singapore, which will be held in Singapore from June 15-17, 2022.

A stamp-sized microfluidic chip measures the concentration of SARS-CoV-2 nucleocapsid protein in blood serum from a standard finger prick.

NASA is set to start high-voltage functional ground testing of the agency's first all-electric X-plane, the X-57 Maxwell.

Hydrazine, a highly toxic fuel used by spacecraft hypergolic thrusters, is dangerous for humans to handle and bad for the environment. Ammonia borane, with its hypergolic properties, could be used as part of a safer hybrid propellant.

4 March 2021. Reports: In Boca Chica, Texas, on Wednesday, 3 March, SpaceX tested another one of its Starship prototypes that it hopes will launch cargo and people to the moon and Mars. Excluding a heavy booster that creates a two-stage system, the reusable rocket stands at about 45 m tall, or about the size of a 15-story building, with a 9 m diameter. The stainless steel vehicle is powered by three Raptor rocket engines, and would be able to carry as many as 100 passengers and 100 metric tons of cargo. The SN10 flight was similar to the ones SpaceX performed in December and February, when it test-flew prototypes SN8 and SN9, respectively. Both rockets completed objectives like testing aerodynamics, shutting down the engines in succession, and flipping to orient for landing, but both prototypes exploded on impact as they failed to slow down enough. SN10 landed successfully yesterday after executing a belly flop maneuver, but the rocket exploded a few minutes later (due to a suspected methane leak).

Researchers at the National Institute of Standards and Technology have developed a method of added manufacturing gels that has the potential to create complex structures with nanometer-scale precision, leading to the development of soft medical devices that can be inserted into the human body.

Researchers, led by a University of Houston engineer, have reported the development of a cardiac patch made from fully rubbery electronics that can be placed directly on the heart to collect electrophysiological activity, temperature, heartbeat, and other indicators, all at the same time.

Sensors that monitor a patient during medical procedures can be expensive, uncomfortable, even dangerous. An international research team has designed a highly sensitive, flexible gas sensor that can be implanted in the body and, when no longer needed, safely biodegrades into materials absorbed by the body.

Wearable devices can identify COVID-19 cases earlier than traditional diagnostic methods, and can help track and improve management of the disease, researchers report in one of the first studies on the topic.

In the future, a wearable (like a sticker on the skin), bioelectronic device could wirelessly transmit a person's vital signs — potentially providing critical information for early detection of health issues, such as COVID-19 or heart disease — to a healthcare provider, eliminating the need for an in-person visit, while also saving lives.

Specialists are working on an algorithm that takes as input various data sources, such as RSS feeds with news and blogs related to a certain industry, and produces an alarm numerical index to be used as an input to a complete forecasting mathematical model.

AI, being data intensive, is affecting the network speed.

Mathematical and digital oncology play significant roles in the oncological efforts.

3D structural-sensing robots are now being developed and tested in order to take on basic healthcare tasks to support the work of doctors and nurses.

Researchers have developed an easy way to make millirobots by coating objects with a glue-like magnetic spray. Driven by the magnetic field, the coated objects can crawl, walk, or roll on different surfaces. As the magnetic coating is biocompatible, this technology demonstrates the potential for biomedical applications, including catheter navigation and drug delivery.

Working with computer simulations, researchers have developed a concept for a soft-bodied robot that can turn rigid on demand. The approach could enable a new generation of robots that combine the strength and precision of rigid robots with the fluidity and safety of soft ones.

A new Department of Energy open-access quantum computing testbed is ready for the public. Scientists from Indiana University recently became the first team to begin using Sandia National Laboratories' Quantum Scientific Computing Open User Testbed, or QSCOUT. Quantum computers are poised to become major technological drivers over the coming decades.

Taking inspiration from origami, MIT engineers have designed a medical patch that can be folded around minimally invasive surgical tools and delivered through airways, intestines, and other narrow spaces to patch up internal injuries. It resembles a paper-like film when dry. Once it makes contact with wet tissues or organs, it transforms into a stretchy gel that sticks to an injured site.

A new kind of wearable device could deliver real-time medical data to those with eye or mouth diseases, according to a Penn State Department of Engineering Science and Mechanics professor.

Researchers have developed a new class of medical instruments to improve the diagnoses and treatments of cardiac diseases. Led by engineers at George Washington University and Northwestern University, they applied stretchable matrices of electrode sensors and actuators, along with temperature and pressure sensors, to a balloon catheter system for minimally invasive surgeries.

Insect-sized drones with unprecedented dexterity and resilience are powered by a new class of soft actuator that allows them to operate in tight spaces and withstand collisions. The tiny drones could be used for search and rescue or for machinery inspections in cramped areas.

As NASA develops plans for increasingly ambitious human missions, including a return to the Moon and, eventually, exploration of Mars, more advanced medical risk assessment is necessary in order to keep astronauts healthy.

Researchers have succeeded in finetuning a new thermoplastic biomaterial to enable both the rate at which it degrades in the body, and its mechanical properties to be controlled independently.

Researchers at the Francis Crick Institute and the University of Western Australia have developed a new imaging method to see where antibiotics have reached bacteria within tissues. The method could be used to help develop more effective antibiotic treatments, reducing the risk of antibiotic resistance.

Cubic zirconia is easy and inexpensive to make, and the diamond industry has long considered it a serious threat. De Beers helped pioneer a new, inexpensive method for testing these small stones, using near infrared and time-gated imaging to tell colorless cubic zirconia from the real deal.

Researchers at the University of Strathclyde have demonstrated that 3D optical imaging for surveillance and robotic applications can be performed with LED lighting and a smartphone, and without complex manual processes to synchronize the camera with the lighting.

University of Cambridge research shows that combining computed tomography scans with ultrasound images can create a visual guide for doctors, to enable them to sample a tumor with fewer biopsies. The technique could even lead to virtual biopsies, sparing patients invasive procedures.

A deep-learning algorithm for designing soft robots optimizes placement of sensors within the robot's body, helping to automate the process of robot design. Better sensor placement could have industrial applications, especially where robots are used for fine tasks like gripping.

Experts are building machine learning and artificial intelligence models for engineering simulations.

New exoskeleton legs make their steps on their own, using sophisticated artificial intelligence. The self-controlled legs may someday support the movements of the elderly and those with physical disabilities.

A chemical process from UC Berkeley turns the plastic bag into a strong adhesive.

A new gauge from NASA could continuously monitor fluid flow in pipes on the International Space Station, and prevent satellites from colliding.

After seven months and about 483 millions of km, the Mars 2020 rover landed on the Red Planet on February 18 for a primary mission span of at least one Martian year (687 Earth days).

For many years, airport operations have relied mainly on voice communications over unsecured radio frequencies, with landline calls as the only secure backup. Now, using new technology, FAA staff in control towers can send safety-critical information digitally and securely.

A method was developed for a swarm of hundreds of small battery-powered drones to autonomously return from missions to unmanned ground vehicles (UGVs) for recharging. Mathematical algorithms are being developed to enable route planning for multiple teams of small unmanned air and ground vehicles.

State-of-the-art high-temperature shielding materials are not flexible; however, a new technology forms the structurally robust, thermally stable boron nitride nanotube (BNNT) into a low-weight, flexible mat.

Cultivating software engineers in medtech is essential.

There are serious failures in AI software if there are bad data in the software.

USA, Boston, 3 Dec 2009, from Avenue Louis Pasteur (1822-1895, French microbiologist), Boston Public Latin School (1635, Schola Latina Bostoniensis, the oldest and the first public exam school in the U.S.).

General news and issues

Uncivilized and unpolite companies are everywhere – people will soon correct this problem.

Some conferences in the week 8 – 12 March include the Deutsche Bank 29th Annual Media, Internet and Telecom Conference;
- the Barclays Global Healthcare Conference including presentations by Moderna and Sarepta Therapeutics;
- the Truist Securities Technology, Internet & Services Conference 2021 including presentations by BigCommerce and Zscaler;
- the Susquehanna 10th Annual Technology Conference;
- the HC Wainwright Global Life Sciences Conference;
- the Baird's Vehicle Technology & Mobility Conference, and
- the Gabelli & Company 12th Annual Specialty Chemicals Conference.

Incompetent people in many companies use bad computer programs, ask customers to update, etc., but the computer programs do not work.

Reports: The climate naturally – not anthropogenetic (or for political reasons) - changed for billions of years, and will continue to naturally – not anthropogenetic - change for a few more billions of years. Only a catastrophic nuclear war would have anthropogenetic climate change, and for this reason all people ask for zero arms. There are frequent devastating wildfires and destructive hurricanes - these natural disasters have grave impacts on people's lives and economy, causing billions of dollars in damages and hundreds of deaths every year, but they are preventable. All classes of extreme events (such as heat waves, drought, coastal flooding, and intense precipitation) are caused or worsened by natural – not anthropogenic - climate sinusoidal changes. For many thousands of years, Moon and Solar eclipses, natural sinusoidal climate changes, natural extreme events, astronomical events, etc., were used by all rulers of the day for their personal ambitions – now, of course, the eclipses, natural extreme events, astronomical events, etc. don't work anymore, but the natural sinusoidal climate changes are still used.

In the Arctic Ocean, the average temperature in March is −25 to −30 degrees Celsius; the ice thickness is up to 1.5 m, with winds up to 115 km/h.

Reports: Amazon.com is developing a chip to power the hardware switches used in networking.

Rome: Accademia Nazionale dei Lincei (1603, the oldest worldwide) has its library in Palazzo Corsini (1740), Via della Lungara 10, Roma.

Aphorisms

No arms = peace + better life.

The more computer updates, the more computer sluggishness.

The more preparations for war, the more unhappiness for people.

History is full of bad events, but there are also many good events – let's focus on the good ones, in order to have peace, zero arms, freedom, good health, good education, good jobs, good science & technology, harmony and prosperity for all.

Arms sap joy from life – elimination of arms will rekindle optimism, self-esteem, renew people's energy and enthusiasm, reconnect people with other people, and help people pursue what they love most.

The desire and preparation for war are treatable and beatable — and people will regain purpose, happiness and peace-of-mind!

Don't let the war mentality steal another day!

Humor

Two ladies have a chat, admiring the Pacific Ocean:
- Many computers are pretty darn flexible, right?
- Oh, yes, but why?
- Probably because they have so many bugs….

Later:
- What you got on Christmas?
- You see, we have very nice neighbors, and we exchanged a few cute little presents. And you?
- Well, one neighbor, just before Christmas, put a public toilet and a big dumpster in front of our house, and started a big construction work.
- Don't say! But they finished by the New Year 2021, right?
- No way, still going after 2 and a half months….
- That's something – but they'll finish soon.
- You are so…
- I know – sexy!

A few days later:
- We have so beautiful trees in our city, and they are well maintained by a company.
- Must be expensive…
- No, actually the company uses the cut branches, and pays the city.
- That's smart! We have beautiful trees too, but many branches are over the roads, ready to fall any second…
- Oh, no, this is dangerous.
- Yes, it was a big wind the other day, and a big branch fell on a car.
- Any injuries?
- No, but the car was smashed.
- Whose car was it?

- Mayor's......

Next day:
- Recently several people addressed very politely to me, and I responded in the same way.
- That's nice, but some addressed to me in writing "Hey".
- This is an insult! And what did you respond?
- Excuse me, do you speak English?
-

Over the weekend:
- Listen, many bureaucrats with power believe that people are cows.
- True, but why?
- To be milked of money.....
- Well, soon the cows will ask for money back....

A young lady and an old one admire the Pacific Ocean. The old one:
- What's new, little girl?
- Too much bureaucracy – and you?
- Well, I cannot run as fast or jump as high as I did when I was a teenager, and my brain's cognitive power — my ability to learn, remember, and solve problems — slows down with age. I find it harder to summon once familiar facts or divide my attention among two or more activities or sources of information.
- What about focus?
- Sure, these changes affect my ability to focus, so I find myself getting more easily distracted than I was when I was like you.
- Hearing issues?
- But of course, hearing loss that often accompanies aging makes it more difficult to distinguish speech in a noisy environment.
- Yes, because hearing then requires more concentration than usual, even mild loss of the ability to focus can affect speech comprehension.
- You see, most people start to notice changes as they enter their 50s and 60s.
- Indeed, although these changes can cause consternation, most age-related memory and thinking problems don't stem from an

underlying brain disease such as Alzheimer's disease. Instead, what appears to be a memory problem may simply reflect a slower processing speed and poor encoding and retrieval of new memories as a result of diminished attention.

- However, even though my brain may be slower to learn and recall new information, my ability to make sense of what I know, and to form reasonable arguments and judgments remains intact.

- That's nice - many of these limitations are reversible and related to poor sleep, but structural changes that take place in our brains as we age can explain some of these developments, too.

- True, brain regions involved with memory processing, such as the hippocampus and especially the frontal lobes, undergo anatomical and neurochemical changes over time.

- Right - the result is that as we age, it takes longer to absorb, process, and remember new information. The natural loss of receptors and neurons that occurs with aging may also make it harder to concentrate.

- Sure, therefore, I not only learn information more slowly, but I also may have more trouble recalling it, because I didn't fully learn it in the first place. With slower processing, facts held in working memory may dissipate before I have had a chance to solve a problem.

- Yes, in addition, the ability to perform tasks that involve executive function declines with age. Many people learn to compensate for these changes by relying on habit most of the time, and devoting extra effort to focus on new information they are trying to learn.

- Certainly, even the aches and pains of getting older can affect focus. Pain itself is distracting, and some of the medications used to treat it also can affect concentration. Therefore, little girl – stay young!

- No, I want to get old like you, and forget everything!

Our Future is Sustainable Peace, Freedom and Prosperity

People want:

NOT kill everything with lasers – people want lasers only to make them healthier

NOT use of space for war

NOT 5G for war

NOT quantum electronic warfare

NOT Mosaic Warfare with AI – people need Mosaic Houses with AI

NOT artificial intelligence (AI) cognitive electronic warfare (EW)

NOT destroyers – only recreation ships

NOT 60-kilowatt laser weapons – only medical laser

NOT drone swarm of mass destruction – only helping drones for families

NOT nuclear missiles – only peaceful rackets for people benefit

NOT attack helicopters – only medical helicopters

NOT hypersonic missiles – only hypersonic passenger planes

NOT air dominance – only air collaboration for people benefits

NOT AI and edge computing for war – only for peace

NOT special war forces – only special medical teams

NOT stabilization technology for infantry rifles – people want stabilization technology for people's health

NOT unmanned tanks – only unmanned vehicles for people assistance

NOT space for war – only space for peace

NOT artillery smart munitions – only medical smart equipment

NOT algorithms and sensors for combat – only algorithms and sensors for better life

NOT AI warfare – AI only for peace

NOT hypersonic weapons – only hypersonic commercial airplanes for better life

NOT war-related industry – only peace-related industry for healthy living

NOT laser weapons – only laser for medical and other peaceful applications

The war-related industry is really sick – people want to transform it into a peace-related industry

People ask to have all war-related platforms transformed in peace and health-related platforms.

All war-related budgets are very sick.

The enemy is not people – the enemy is the virus.

Germany, 22 March 1978, Dortmund, the store Besta Hungshans (left), Avis rental service (center).

Bibliography

"The Histories" by Polybius
"Discours de la Méthode" by René Descartes
"Meditationes de prima philosophia" by René Descartes
"Philosophiae Naturalis Principia Mathematica" by Isaac Newton
Chinese encyclopedia Gujin Tushu Jicheng (Imperial Encyclopedia)
"Encyclopédie" by Jean-Baptiste le Rond d'Alembert and Denis Diderot
"Encyclopaedia Britannica" by over 4,400 contributors
"Encyclopedia Americana" by Francis Lieber
"Invent and Wander" by Jeff Bezos
Other sources include: UPI, Nature, CNBC, AP, Nasdaq, AAAS, Reuters, EDGAR, AFP, Recode, Europa Press, American Mathematical Society, Bloomberg News, Fox News, USA, Deutsche Presse-Agentur, MSNBC, BBC, Australian Associated Press, Agência Brasil, The Canadian Press (La Presse Canadienne), Middle East News Agency, Baltic News Service, Suomen Tietotoimisto, Athens-Macedonian News Agency, Asian News International, Inter Press Service, Kyodo News, Notimex, Algemeen Nederlands Persbureau, AGERPRES, Newsis, Tidningarnas Telegrambyrå, Swiss Telegraphic Agency, Central News Agency, ANKA news agency, Agenzia Fides

Michael M. Dediu is also the author of these books (which can be found on Amazon.com, and www.derc.com):

1. Aphorisms and quotations – with examples and explanations
2. Axioms, aphorisms and quotations – with examples and explanations
3. 100 Great Personalities and their Quotations
4. Professor Petre P. Teodorescu – A Great Mathematician and Engineer
5. Professor Ioan Goia – A Dedicated Engineering Professor
6. Venice (Venezia) – a new perspective. A short presentation with photographs

7. La Serenissima (Venice) - a new photographic perspective. A short presentation with many photos

8. Grand Canal – Venice. A new photographic viewpoint. A short presentation with many photos

9. Piazza San Marco – Venice. A different photographic view. A short presentation with many photos

10. Roma (Rome) - La Città Eterna. A new photographic view. A short presentation with many photos

11. Why is Rome so Fascinating? A short presentation with many photos

12. Rome, Boston and Helsinki. A short photographic presentation

13. Rome and Tokyo – two captivating cities. A short photographic presentation

14. Beautiful Places on Earth – A new photographic presentation

15. From Niagara Falls to Mount Fuji via Rome - A novel photographic presentation

16. From the USA and Canada to Italy and Japan - A fresh photographic presentation

Paris: Université Paris 1 Panthéon-Sorbonne (1971, after the division of the University of Paris (Sorbonne, 1150)), on Rue Saint-Jacques (left) and Rue Soufflot (right, to Panthéon (1758 – 1790)).

17. Paris – Why So Many Call This City Mon Amour - A lovely photographic presentation

18. The City of Light – Paris (La Ville-Lumière) - A kaleidoscopic photographic presentation

19. Paris (Lutetia Parisiorum) – the romance capital of the world - A kaleidoscopic photographic view

20. Paris and Tokyo – a joyful photographic presentation. With a preamble about the Universe

21. From USA to Japan via Canada – A cheerful photographic documentary

22. 200 Wonderful Places, In The Last 50 Years – A personal photographic documentary

23. Must see places in USA and Japan - A kaleidoscopic photographic documentary

24. Grandeurs of the World - A kaleidoscopic photographic documentary

25. Corneliu Leu – writer on the same wavelength as Mark Twain. An American viewpoint

26. From Berkeley to Pompeii via Rome – A kaleidoscopic photographic documentary

27. From America to Europe via Japan - A kaleidoscopic photographic documentary

28. Discover America and Japan - A photographic documentary

29. J. R. Lucas – philosopher on a creative parallel with Plato, An American viewpoint

30. From America to Switzerland via France - A photographic documentary

31. From Bretton Woods to New York via Cape Cod - A photographic documentary

32. Splendid Places on the Atlantic Coast of the U. S. A. - A photographic documentary

33. Fourteen nice Cities on three Continents - A photographic documentary

34. 17 Picturesque Cities on the World Map - A photographic documentary

35. Unforgettable Places from Four Continents, including Trump buildings - A photographic documentary

36. Dediu Newsletter, Volume 1, Number 1, 6 December 2016 – Monthly news, review, comments and suggestions for a better and wiser world
37. Dediu Newsletter, Volume 1, Number 2, 6 January 2017 (available also at www.derc.com).
38. Dediu Newsletter, Volume 1, Number 3, 6 February 2017 (available at www.derc.com).
39. London and Greenwich, - A photographic documentary
40. Dediu Newsletter, Volume 1, Number 4, 6 March 2017 (available also at www.derc.com).
41. Dediu Newsletter, Volume 1, Number 5, 6 April 2017 (available also at www.derc.com).
42. Dediu Newsletter, Volume 1, Number 6, 6 May 2017 (available also at www.derc.com).
43. Dediu Newsletter, Volume 1, Number 7, 6 June 2017 (available also at www.derc.com).
44. London, Oxford and Cambridge, A photographic documentary
45. Dediu Newsletter, Volume 1, Number 8, 6 July 2017 (available also at www.derc.com).
46. Dediu Newsletter, Volume 1, Number 9, 6 August 2017 (available also at www.derc.com).

USA, Cambridge, 23 September 2009, on the campus of Harvard University (1636) in Cambridge, The Harry Elkins Widener (1885-1912 (died on Titanic)) Memorial Library (1915, Beaux-Arts architecture, 3.5 M of books).

47. Dediu Newsletter, Volume 1, Number 10, 6 September 2017 (available also at www.derc.com).

48. Three Great Professors: President Woodrow Wilson, Historian German Arciniegas, and Mathematician Gheorghe Vranceanu – A chronological and photographic documentary

49. Dediu Newsletter, Volume 1, Number 11, 6 October 2017 (available also at www.derc.com).

50. Dediu Newsletter, Volume 1, Number 12, 6 November 2017 (available also at www.derc.com).

51. Dediu Newsletter, Volume 2, Number 1 (13), 6 December 2017 (available also at www.derc.com).

52. Two Great Leaders: Augustus and George Washington - A chronological and photographic documentary

53. Dediu Newsletter, Volume 2, Number 2 (14), 6 January 2018 (available also at www.derc.com).

54. Newton, Benjamin Franklin, and Gauss, A chronological and photographic documentary

55. Dediu Newsletter, Volume 2, Number 3 (15), 6 February 2018 (available also at www.derc.com).

56. 2017: World Top Events, But Many Little Known, A chronological and photographic documentary

57. Dediu Newsletter, Volume 2, Number 4 (16), 6 March 2018 (available also at www.derc.com).

58. Vergilius, Horatius, Ovidius, and Shakespeare - A chronological and photographic documentary.

59. Dediu Newsletter, Volume 2, Number 5 (17), 6 April 2018 (available also at www.derc.com).

60. Dediu Newsletter, Volume 2, Number 6 (18), 6 May 2018 (available also at www.derc.com).

61. Vivaldi, Bach, Mozart, and Verdi - A chronological and photographic documentary.

62. Dediu Newsletter, Volume 2, Number 7 (19), 6 June 2018 (available also at www.derc.com).

63. Dediu Newsletter, Volume 2, Number 8 (20), 6 July 2018 (available also at www.derc.com).

64. Dediu Newsletter, Volume 2, Number 9 (21), 6 August 2018 (available also at www.derc.com).

65. World History, a new perspective - A chronological and photographic documentary.

66. World Humor History with over 100 Jokes, a new perspective - A chronological and photographic documentary

67. Dediu Newsletter, Volume 2, Number 10 (22), 6 September 2018 (available also at www.derc.com).

68. Dediu Newsletter, Volume 2, Number 11 (23), 6 October 2018 (available also at www.derc.com).

69. Dediu Newsletter, Volume 2, Number 12 (24), 6 November 2018

70. Da Vinci, Michelangelo, Rembrandt, Rodin - A chronological and photographic documentary

71. Dediu Newsletter, Volume 3, Number 1 (25), 6 December 2018

72. Dediu Newsletter, Volume 3, Number 2 (26), 6 January 2019

73. From Euclid to Edison – revelries in the past 75 years - A chronological and photographic documentary

74. – Socrates to Churchill Aphorisms celebrated after 1960 - A chronological and photographic documentary

UK, London: the upper part of the western façade and entrance of Westminster Abbey (960, 1517, Anglican abbey with daily services, and all coronations since 1066, tower height 69 m).

75. - Dediu Newsletter, Volume 3, Number 3 (27), 6 February 2019

76. – Hippocrates to Fleming: Medicine History celebrated after 1943 - A chronological and photographic documentary

77. - Dediu Newsletter, Volume 3, Number 4 (28), 6 March 2019

78. - Dediu Newsletter, Volume 3, Number 5 (29), 6 April 2019

79 – Archimedes to Ford: Invention History celebrated after 1943 - A chronological and photographic documentary

80 - Dediu Newsletter, Volume 3, Number 6 (30), 6 May 2019

81 – Sutherland to Pavarotti: Great Singers History - A chronological and photographic documentary

82 - Dediu Newsletter, Volume 3, Number 7 (31), 6 June 2019

83 - Dediu Newsletter, Volume 3, Number 8 (32), 6 July 2019

84 – Augustus to Rockefeller: History of the Wealthiest People - A chronological and photographic documentary

85 - Dediu Newsletter, Volume 3, Number 9 (33), 6 August 2019

86 – Pythagoras to Fermi: History of Science - A chronological and photographic documentary

87 - Dediu Newsletter, Volume 3, Number 10 (34), 6 September 2019

88 – Our Future is Sustainable Peace and Prosperity – Moving from conflicts to harmony and peace

89 - Dediu Newsletter, Volume 3, Number 11 (35), 6 October 2019 – World Monthly Report with news

90 – Our Future Depends on Good World Educations – Moving from frail education to solid education

91 - Dediu Newsletter, Volume 3, Number 12 (36), 6 November 2019 – World Monthly Report with News and Suggestions for Sustainable Peace, Freedom and Prosperity

92 – Friendly, Helpful & Smart World Management - Moving from bureaucracy to responsive world management

93 – If You Want Peace, Prepare for Peace! – Moving from preparation for war to preparation for peace

94 - Dediu Newsletter, Volume 4, Number 1 (37), 6 December 2019 – World Monthly Report with News and Suggestions for Sustainable Peace, Freedom and Prosperity

95 – World with One Country & its Ten Friendly Regions - Moving from 195 disagreeing countries, to 1 country with 10 collaborating regions

96 - Dediu Newsletter, Volume 4, Number 2 (38), 6 January 2020 – World Monthly Report with News and Suggestions for Sustainable Peace, Freedom and Prosperity

97 – After 10,000 Years of Conflicts, People want 10,000 Years of Harmony - Moving from continuous wars to stable peace

98 - Dediu Newsletter, Volume 4, Number 3 (39), 6 February 2020 – World Monthly Report with News and Suggestions for Sustainable Peace, Freedom and Prosperity

99 – The Constitution of the World – Moving from many unsustainable constitutions, to just one Constitution of the World

100 - Dediu Newsletter, Volume 4, Number 4 (40), 6 March 2020 – World Monthly Report with News and Suggestions for Sustainable Peace, Freedom and Prosperity

101 - Dediu Newsletter, Volume 4, Number 5 (41), 6 April 2020 – World Monthly Report

102 - Dediu Newsletter, Volume 4, Number 6 (42), 6 May 2020 – World Monthly Report

103 – World Constitution Implementation – Moving from violent changes, to smooth transition to the Constitution of the World

104 - Dediu Newsletter, Volume 4, Number 7 (43), 6 June 2020 – World Monthly Report

105 - Dediu Newsletter, Volume 4, Number 8 (44), 6 July 2020 – World Monthly Report

106 - It is getting truer and truer – we urgently need the World Constitution: Moving from anarchic changes, to balanced transition to the Constitution of the World

107 - Dediu Newsletter, Volume 4, Number 9 (45), 6 August 2020 – World Monthly Report

108 - World Constitution with Lovely Comments - Moving from many suboptimal constitutions to the much better Constitution of the World

109 - Dediu Newsletter, Volume 4, Number 10 (46), 6 September 2020 – World Monthly Report

110 – World Constitution with Questions & Answers – Moving from many obsolete constitutions to the much better Constitution of the World

111 - Dediu Newsletter, Volume 4, Number 11 (47), 6 October 2020 – World Monthly Report

112 - World Projects - Moving from minor projects to great projects for the World

113 - Dediu Newsletter, Volume 4, Number 12 (48), 6 November 2020 – World Monthly Report

114 - Dediu Newsletter, Volume 5, Number 1 (49), 6 December 2020 – World Monthly Report

115 - World Opportunities for All - Moving from few local jobs, to world opportunities for all

116 - Dediu Newsletter, Volume 5, Number 2 (50), 6 January 2021 – World Monthly Report

117 - Self-Managing World - Moving from local ruling top-down, to self-managing world

USA, Boston (1630): Charles River Basin (water flowing from left to right, into Atlantic Ocean), with Longfellow Bridge (1900-1906, 539 m) carrying Route 3 and the Red Line metro between Boston (down, Lederman Park (right)) and Cambridge (up, MIT (left)).

118 – We are all in the same space boat – Peaceful Terra; Moving from local fragile boats to the solid Peaceful Terra
119 - Dediu Newsletter, Volume 5, Number 3 (51), 6 February 2021 – World Monthly Report
120 - All people ask for Peace + Freedom = Prosperity, Moving from local conflicts to world peace and freedom
121 - Dediu Newsletter, Volume 5, Number 4 (52), 6 March 2021 – World Monthly Report
122 - To pour Peace from a cup full of arms, MELT ALL ARMS! - Moving from arms race, to peace enjoyment

Mathematical Reviews: American Mathematical Society (AMS) sent for review, over the years, 304 mathematical research papers and books, to Michael M. Dediu, and his reviews were published in the Mathematical Reviews of the AMS.

Italy, Rome: The Temple of Vesta and Rome and a flag throwing festival on 8 December 2011.

www.ingramcontent.com/pod-product-compliance
Lightning Source LLC
Chambersburg PA
CBHW041713200326
41519CB00001B/143